What are readers saying?

Grandparenting on Purpose is a wonderful guide for anyone lucky enough to have grandchildren. The best grandparents offer children love, respect, guidance, and fun. This book offers instruction and inspiration in all these areas.

Mary Pipher, PhD
Clinical Psychologist
Recipient of the American Psychological Association's
Presidential Citation
Award-Winning Author of *Reviving Ophelia:*
Saving the Selves of Adolescent Girls

From the introductory pages which set the tone for the book, I was relieved to find that this would be a safe, comfortable book for me to read. This book wasn't going to be a recitation of what a grandparent should and should not do. Each chapter of the book discusses principles that can be applied in *every* family with ideas for exploring ways to identify, connect, and expand family bonds.

Trisha Stoker
Grandmother of Twenty-Seven

This book shares many delightful, fun, and profound examples, while, at the same time, encouraging and empowering us to create our own style of "grandparenting on purpose." Thank you, Winn and Linda, for writing this book that grandparents will refer to time and time again for inspiration and motivation.

Betsy Folland
Parent Educator, The Road Home
Grandmother of Four

This is a book filled with joy and wisdom. I dare any grandparent to not find dozens of practical and inspiring ways to enrich your relationship with your grandchildren. Just make sure you pay attention to the authors' plea not to compare yourself with them. They are like grandparent athletes who can help the rest of us improve our game!

William J. Doherty, PhD
Professor of Family Social Science, University of Minnesota
Cofounder of Braver Angels

Winn and Linda provide a powerful and practical workbook for all grandparents who want to make a difference with their grandchildren. The book delivers insights and suggestions for almost every situation and personality grandparents may encounter.

Dan and Carol Ellertson
Grandparents of Twenty-Nine

Overall, I just really loved the entire book. Your ideas and activities were so fun and creative and there is an obvious free flow that goes on in your household. We can all aspire to have these beautiful, joyful tenets in our households that can be carried on from generation to generation!

Vera Naputi, MS
AVID teacher and Instructional Coach
East High School
Madison Metropolitan School District

Whether you have one grandchild or many grandchildren, you will add depth to your relationships by considering some of the many ways Winn and Linda Egan have been extraordinary grandparents. . . . Any grandparent wanting to have a more positive impact on his or her grandchildren will find a treasure trove of possibilities in Winn and Linda Egan's very personal book.

David S. Folland, MD, Pediatrician
Grandparent of Four

Grandparenting on Purpose is the 21st Century equivalent to Dr. Spock's landmark parenting book from the 1950s. It is the "go-to" resource for all grandparents who endeavor to establish and maintain loving and purposeful relationships with their grandchildren. Its conversational voice engages the reader with an array of topics and themes that include easy-to-follow steps and guides to activities that will enrich the lives of grandparents and the grandchildren they love.

Marshall Welch, PhD, D.Min.
Grandfather of Two

Winn and Linda probably did a good job with their children, but they are doing an even better job with their grandchildren. . . . After reading Winn and Linda's book on grandparenting you will wish they had been your grandparents. But you will also discover great ideas about how to be grandparents like them.

Cordell Jacobson, PhD
Grandfather of Twelve

GRANDPARENTING
on PURPOSE

GRANDPARENTING
on PURPOSE

Fresh Ideas, Activities, and Traditions
for Connecting with
Grandchildren Near and Far

M. WINSTON EGAN & LINDA EGAN

WinnPrint Publishing
Millcreek, Utah

Editorial work by Eschler Editing
Cover design by MiblArt
Illustrations by Thomas Tolman (tolmanstudio.com)
Interior print design and layout by Marny K. Parkin
Ebook design and layout by Marny K. Parkin
Production services facilitated by Scrivener Books

 Published by WinnPrint Publishing

ISBN 978-1-949165-25-8

To our wonderful grandchildren, their loving parents,
our parents, our grandparents, and dear friends

 **Contents**

"Young people need something stable to hang on to—a culture connection, a sense of their own past, a hope for their own future. Most of all, they need what grandparents can give them."

Dr. Jay Kesler

Past President and Chancellor of Taylor University

 # Acknowledgments

Forever, I will be indebted to my companion and helpmeet, Linda, for her contributions to my life as a husband, father, and grandfather. In so many ways, she is the genius behind the ideas, traditions, and practices revealed in *Grandparenting on Purpose*. We profoundly miss her and her loving influence.

From Linda's earliest years as a child to the end of her life, she was a remarkable light and example to all—friends, work associates, cousins, aunts and uncles, and everyone. Her goodness was unrivaled and constant. Our children, their spouses, and grandchildren loved and respected her. When they were in her presence, they felt her deep and sustaining love.

I am also indebted to Linda's grandmother, Rhoda Griffin Dahle, who played such a vital role in nurturing her during her youthful years. She was the kind of grandparent Linda and I aspired to be.

Also, I wish to acknowledge the profound influence of my parents, Merritt, and Marcia Egan. They played a central role in caring for our children. Their connection to them was affirming and sustaining. They, too, were superb examples of capable and caring grandparenting.

I express sincere appreciation to life-long friends and loving relatives who have blessed our lives as parents and grandparents— Steve and Linda Wright, Brent and Marilyn Gandre, Les and Dianne Feil, Rosemary and Jack Wixom, Warren and Suzanne Tate, Becky and Jamie Cannon, Steve and Tricia Stoker, DeAnna and Lynn DeBry, Shonnie and Richard Scott, Jeff and Kathy Anderson, David and Neill Marriott, Betsy and David Folland, Sheril and Dianne Torgerson, Steven and Roxanne Shallenberger, Julie and Craig Berry, Nancy and George Hansen, McKinley and Leslie Osward, Carol and Daniel Ellertson, Joseph and Dixie Cannon, Randall and Sharon Harmsen, Julie and Kit Romney, Joann and James Young, Romney and Mary Sue Burk, Douglas and Sharon Bliss, Kaye and Lynn Wallace, Joe and Ginny Cannon, Carla Cannon, Kathleen Slagle, Marian Yates, Judy and Joseph Mansey, as well as Art and Luana Casper. I express deep appreciation to the Eschler Editing Team and associates: Angela Eschler, Shanda Cottam, Desiree Johns, Melissa Dalton Martinez, Kathy Jenkins Oveson, Michele Preisendorf, Chris Bigelow, Heidi Brockbank, Marny K. Parkin, and Alysha Rummler. Each contributed significantly and painstakingly to the publishing process and the finalization of the book. Also, I am deeply grateful for the superb illustrations and icons created by Thomas Tolman.

I would be remiss if I did not thank our children and their spouses: Daniel and Kristin Egan, Amy and Scott Harmer, Mary and Ryan Fuhriman, and Marcia and David Peterson. They have been some of our best teachers as well as our best students. We love them dearly and so much appreciate their patience and kindness in accepting our sincere attempts to be purposeful grandparents.

Finally, I thank each of our grandchildren and where appropriate their spouses (Ben, Hannah, Skyler, Emma, Sam, Esther, Tanette, Matt, Gabe, Davidson, Noah, McKinzie, Eliza, Sam, Mary Jane, Winston, Jake, Maggie, Ellie, Livie, Rosie, Elizabeth, Mika, Abby, Rebekah, and Dane) for putting up with us. They have taught me so much! I love each of them dearly. I know Linda loves them deeply too.

M. Winston Egan

 # Foreword

We are the grandparents of 28 grandchildren and five great-grandchildren. They range in age from 2 months old to 26 years old. They are diverse in many ways. We have a granddaughter from China, and two grandchildren from Tonga. We face together many health challenges, mostly autoimmune related: Graves Disease, Celiac Disease, Lupus, Rheumatoid Arthritis, and Lyme Disease. Also, we share a gene that makes one prone to Melanoma and Pancreatic Cancer. Just recently, we had a great-granddaughter diagnosed with Cystic Fibrosis. We mention this to express how we have grown as a family as we have supported each other in positively approaching challenges knowing that we can do hard things well.

We get what it means to be "grandparents on purpose!" Grandparenting is a priority in our lives. We spend a great deal of our time relating to and connecting with our grandchildren and their parents. This calling, which we genuinely believe this is, is the major thrust of our "senior" years. We are committed to the happiness of our grandchildren and their parents. Thus, we take the opportunities we have to be with them very seriously and to contribute to their well-being. It turns out that we find grandparenting to be immensely rewarding, even though it is challenging. We know this from our own experiences.

When Winn and Linda invited us to write the forward for their book, we were thrilled to comment on their decades-long attempts to be committed and intentional grandparents. For years we have shared thoughts, memories and the joys of grandparenting. We have admired their creativity and influence in shaping the next generation of parents and grandparents.

The book presents valuable and timely ideas for building relationships with grandchildren and engaging them in activities that make a difference in their lives—now and in the future. It is replete with family-tested ideas about discovering the needs of grandchildren and their parents, building fun and meaningful traditions and routines, contributing to the spirituality of grandchildren and supporting talent development.

The book is well organized and easy to read. It focuses on providing readers with ideas they may personalize and adapt to their family conditions and dynamics.

Winn and Linda take specific steps to encourage readers to stay away from comparisons with their practices. They are not interested in making others feel guilty or inadequate. The focus of their recommendations is on growing and changing—becoming the best grandparents you can be—one step at a time.

As experienced and committed grandparents, we gained much from the read of this book. We recommend it highly to anyone who wants to grow as a grandparent. As our children and their spouses move slowly into their grandparenting years, this will certainly be a book we will share with them.

Mac and Leslie Oswald

Preface

Some time ago, dear friends Richard and Shonnie Scott invited us to speak to their empty nester's group about our experiences as grandparents. We were thrilled with this invitation and did our best to prepare thoroughly for the evening. The empty nesters seemed to be genuinely interested in the ideas and practices we shared that evening.

When we reflected on our preparations and the presentation, we thought a book about grandparenting might be useful. We began the writing process within days. Since then, invaluable help has been kindly and competently provided by Richard and Shonnie Scott, Dr. Robert V. Bullough, Dr. Dean Hughes, Steven Shallenberger, Diane Ward, and Julie Young. We so much appreciate their invaluable input and insightful suggestions.

Initially, we used the adjective *deliberate* to describe our grandparenting efforts. However, after some pondering and puttering with other words, we determined that *purposeful* was a more fitting adjective for describing our work. To be purposeful is to be focused and intentional in your grandparenting. You are clear about what you are trying to contribute to your grandchildren's happiness and how you hope to be useful to them and their parents.

We have tried to make the content of this book easy to understand and motivational. We want to have a friendly conversation with you—almost as if we were talking informally with you as a close friend. We want you to feel comfortable in exploring the ideas, practices, and principles that have been so helpful and valuable to us. Also, we want you to be motivated by the stories, examples, and ideas presented in the book, using what you discover to enrich the lives of your grandchildren and their parents.

As you will soon discover, we are exceedingly atypical in our pursuits as grandparents—maybe even a little over the top. That's just who we are. With this confession behind us, here are a few recommendations. Use the book's content as a springboard to design your own unique family activities and traditions. Think about what really makes sense for your family and the needs of your grandchildren and their parents. Use your discoveries to create your own personal style of grandparenting. Have fun learning and growing as a grandparent.

You may read the book sequentially cover to cover, or you may want to use it as an idea or reference book. Or you may want to combine elements of both approaches. There are advantages to each. Just enjoy yourself!

Thumb through the pages to get a feel for this book's layout, structure, and sequencing. Look for statements and questions that naturally catch your attention and interest.

Okay—you are now ready to begin your exploration. Do all the things you did during your school years to heighten your learning and keep your motivation high. Take notes, bend page corners, mark passages, write in the margins, and slow down when the content seems to be dense or a little hard to understand! Stay awake and alert. Our intent is not to put you to sleep. Talk to others about what you are learning and feeling—anything that helps you master the information and capture the ideas presented. Also, begin to test and apply the concepts you find compelling and worthy of trying.

We suggest you use the book as a catalyst for creating or enriching your own skills and practices as a grandparent. Again, this is your opportunity to create and build your own unique traditions, routines, and family events. Not everything you discover will apply to you and your family. However, we believe you will find much that will be both stimulating and helpful. Actively look for ideas that really speak to you. Use the workbook format at the end of each chapter to solidify your thoughts and identify the practices you wish to try and potentially adopt. And remember: enjoy yourself! Have some fun!

Chapter 1

The Heart of Grandparenting on Purpose

We are Winston and Linda Egan. You should know that we are extreme when it comes to being grandparents, which will become abundantly clear as you move through the book. Please don't let that get in the way of your learning and growing. Simply say to yourself, "We could never be this intense!" Focus on ideas, practices, and approaches that fit you and your family.

This book represents our best efforts over the past twenty-five years to positively influence the lives of those we love most—our grandchildren and their parents. As you will discover, we've included essential principles and practices that contribute to the development and sustaining of loving and caring relationships. We believe the establishment of these positive relationships is at the heart of *Grandparenting on Purpose*. The book is all about engendering happiness in your grandchildren and their parents.

Throughout the book, you will discover concrete ways to contribute to your grandchildren and their parents' happiness and success. You will also find beneficial ideas and practices for supporting them as they move through each vital phase of their lives. You will come to understand the whys and hows of making a difference in the lives of those individuals you love so much.

Treat this book as a springboard for you and your family. Use the ideas and practices to shape and develop your own personal approach to connecting with your grandchildren and their parents. As you move through the book, continually ask yourself how can I adapt, modify, and personalize the concepts and approaches for my extended family. Also, think about your children, their spouses, and your grandchildren. What would work with them? What would they thoroughly enjoy doing? Again, we want the book to serve as a catalyst for you. We want you to be empowered to design your own grandparenting style, practices, traditions, and routines.

Our advice is simply this: Look for ideas and practices that resonate with *you* and *your family*. Don't compare yourselves to us; simply search for what makes sense to you.

Our Brief Story

We grew up within several blocks of each other, attending nearby high schools. From our youthful years to the present, we have strived to honor our faith with devotion and consistency. One of these traditions is treating others kindly and compassionately—which includes loving others, especially family members. We believe that much, if not most, of our happiness and purpose in life, is tied to honoring this fundamental conviction.

We have been married for fifty-three years. We have been blessed with four children: Daniel, Amy, Mary, and Marcia. They and their spouses (Kristin, Scott, Ryan, and David) have blessed us with twenty-two grandchildren, five of whom are now married.

As we neared the completion of this book, Linda became extremely ill. She passed away due to the complications of several challenging medical conditions. She had been burdened with constant pain for many years; her passing left us heartbroken, but we are confident she is in a far better place where she is free of pain. The last three weeks of her life were tender and deeply spiritual for all of us. We miss her dearly.

I want this book to serve as a legacy to her remarkable capacities and qualities as a wife, mother, and grandmother. She was and is the genius and architect behind most of our prized family traditions, routines, and practices.

Before Linda's passing, she described her growing-up years and her family. Her reflections speak to the remarkable power and influence of a caring and sensitive grandmother, Grandma Rhoda. She made a gigantic difference in her life.

Linda's Reflections

I grew up in a family of five, the youngest of three girls. Economically, my family was humble. Our family income was used primarily to purchase food, pay the mortgage, buy gas, and pay for other essentials. At a relatively early age, I learned to work hard to pay for personal and other expenses my parents could not provide.

When I was about eight years old, I became aware of problems in my parents' relationship, many of which were connected to my father's significant challenges with alcoholism. His difficulties with this disease affected me in many ways. He could not keep a job. I knew I could not trust or count on him as a father. His behaviors were frequently unpredictable and frightening.

Fortunately, my maternal grandmother lived in a basement apartment of our home. She was not only a caring grandmother, but she also became my counselor—my trusted advisor.

Grandma Rhoda greeted me each day when I came home from school. She was a pretty good cook and often made cakes or cookies to enjoy after returning from school. She often gave me a little money to go to the grocery store to buy small treats.

When I was with my Grandma Rhoda, I felt safe and loved. She sensed the trauma and disappointment I was experiencing. She was there for me. She listened and listened again. She was genuinely interested in what I was feeling and how I spent my school days. She made an enormous difference in my life. I will be forever grateful for her active involvement during my teenage and early young-adult years. Her love was authentic and remarkably sustaining.

I began to date Winn shortly after he finished his service as a missionary in Germany. I came to know he was someone I could trust completely. He came from a family that functioned in healthy and happy ways. His father, Merritt, became the dad I had always wanted and needed. He was kind, understanding, and compassionate. He was dependable. When he made promises, he kept them. He was extraordinarily helpful to our children and me.

Winn and I clearly came from very different family cultures. Our experiences growing up were very dissimilar. However, we successfully blended the best practices of each of our families as we established our own.

Winn and I know grandparents can make a difference in the lives of their grandchildren. We feel impressed to share our experiences and ideas with you, hoping we might inspire you to be more purposeful in your work and calling as a grandparent. We present our stories hoping you may discover useful ideas and practices for becoming and being a more purposeful grandparent.

My Reflections

I have been a professional educator all my life. I have had the privilege of teaching children, youth, and adults of all ages—preschool through graduate school. I have also had the privilege of working with children and youth with behavior disorders and other disabilities.

I grew up as the eldest in a family of eleven children—seven boys and four girls. My mother and father were remarkable parents and grandparents. Most of our married lives, Linda and I lived next door to them—a mere twenty feet from their front door. We loved living near them. As grandparents, they profoundly blessed the lives of our children. They also provided excellent examples of what it meant to be purposeful grandparents.

Our Children and Their Families

All our children are married and live reasonably close to us. Because we live near one another, we have many opportunities to be together for holidays, birthdays, and other celebrations. Like all families, we have our share of challenges, including depression, anxiety, and other health-related conditions. We have also struggled with different issues common to teens—car accidents, acne, drama with friends, curfews, dance preparations, extreme food preferences, and much more.

Our oldest son, Daniel, and his wife, Kristin, have eight children—three biological (a boy and two girls) and five adopted children from Haiti (a set of twin boys, two girls, and another boy). Three of their children are married. Recently, one of the twins, who is now fifteen, spoke about the balance of power in his family. He said to his parents, "There are five of us and five of you." His expression sounded like a statement that one might hear in a western or an adventure movie. However, nothing serious has come from his declaration. Nonetheless, it represented at that moment in time, his thinking about the composition and look of his/their family.

Our first daughter, Amy, and her husband, Scott, have five children—a married son, two daughters, and two additional sons. The oldest daughter recently graduated from college. The youngest daughter is a high school student. Their second, oldest son is a college-age student. Their youngest child, a baby boy, died in utero. His passing caused us to think deeply about a lot of things. Supporting those we love most in times of profound need was a sacred privilege for us as grandparents.

Our second daughter, Mary Ann, and her husband, Ryan, have five children—a son and four daughters. They have a college-age son and daughter, two high school students, and one middle school student. They live very close to us—a mere ten feet from our front door. As of this date, everything is going well. We share eggs and other commodities when needed, bring in one another's mail, and move *Amazon* packages from one doorstep to another. They are phenomenal neighbors.

Our youngest daughter and her husband have four children. Their oldest daughter is married and just finished her bachelor's degree. Their remaining daughters are also college-age students. Their son is a high school student. They have a dog named Chester. When the dog arrived as a puppy, he had a patch of white fur on his "chest." Dane, the youngest child, frequently spoke about the puppy's "chest hair," inspiring the name *Chester*. This brief story about the dog's naming reveals the fun and amusement grandparents may experience if they listen carefully and closely observe what is happening in their grandchildren's lives.

One last note of clarification: Throughout most of the book, *we* use the operative word we to describe our work and calling together. When you encounter an *I*, it refers to me, Grandpa Winn. Also, we use a light-bulb icon 💡 to draw attention to the stories and ideas we have found especially useful—stories and ideas that have had a big impact on us and our grandchildren.

Jump in! Enjoy yourself! Have a growth mindset! Look for what makes sense for you and your family. Remember, the book is your personal springboard for creating your own unique family traditions, routines, and practices.

As we begin our journey together, we want to share what Tanette, one of our dear granddaughters, said about many of the essential features of *Grandparenting on Purpose*.

> I didn't have grandparents in my life for thirteen years. I didn't know what it was like to have grandparents who cared about me and loved me as much as my current grandparents. One thing that my grandparents do that I really love is that they are involved in each grandchild's life. I would say that they are some of my best friends. I have the kind of relationship with them that I feel like I can tell them anything, and I wouldn't feel judged by them. Being good grandparents means you are a friend. I have someone who will listen to me. I have someone who really wants to understand me and who will always be there for me. They love me, unconditionally. That's what my grandparents have been for the last six years that I have been here in America.
>
> *Tanette, Granddaughter, 19*

What Is *Grandparenting on Purpose?*

Grandparenting on purpose is about being engaged in your grandchildren's lives. Whether you live close or reside hundreds or thousands of miles away from your grandkids, you know what they are doing. You are aware of their challenges. You know what they like and love. Simply stated, you determine what they need, and you strive to be genuinely helpful and responsible in responding to their needs. Your calling is to become one of their oldest, most trusted, and wisest friends and advisors.

Grandparenting on purpose is about forming and sustaining enduring relationships with those you love most—your grandchildren and their parents. It is about making a difference in the lives of your grandchildren. You make a difference by being purposeful in your actions.

Your success in contributing to grandkids' happiness and success is deeply rooted in the quality of the relationships you form and sustain over time. Thus, you focus most of your initial work on developing relationships that are positive and lasting. Once these high-quality relationships are in place, you are positioned to be useful and helpful to your grandchildren and their parents.

If your grandkids don't like or trust you, if they don't want to be around you or don't enjoy talking to you or being with you, you will not have much success in supporting and helping or encouraging them. At the heart of "Grandparenting on Purpose" is growing and sustaining positive relationships with your grandchildren and their parents.

You build these positive relationships by coming to know each family member well. You begin to understand their needs. You discover the challenges they face. You know what is genuinely helpful to them. You don't impose your help or lecture them. You know what they are good at and what they like to do. You know what they are currently working on, what they are trying to master, and what they are attempting to learn. You use your knowledge to give positive feedback, provide encouragement, reinforce healthy behaviors, give counsel when invited, and offer proper support as needed.

> Good grandparents are involved in their grandchildren's lives. They are always there for them. They love them and feel their struggles. Also, they bake cookies for them—oatmeal raisin cookies!
>
> *Matt, Grandson, 15*

Let's Get Going

We hope you are eager to discover and explore some of the ideas and practices of *Grandparenting on Purpose*, so we'll dispense with providing a lot of additional theoretical information at this point. You can access this information a little later at the end of this chapter. Here are a few representative samples or ideas to get you engaged and motivated to begin your explorations.

Affirming and Engaging Birthday Letters. One of our favorite practices is writing birthday letters for each of our grandkids and their parents (see chapters 5 and 8 for more details). At the end of each month, we hold a dinner/birthday celebration for all grandkids and their parents, who had birthdays during the month. We enjoy a great dinner together with foods grandkids love and often request. After dinner, we distribute individual birthday letters, followed by the usual singing, cake, candles, and ice cream.

The purposes of these letters are many. First and foremost, they recognize recent achievements or growth. These might

Birthday Letter for a Young Grandson

Dear _____,

I hope you know how much I enjoy being with you and seeing you in action. You are one totally cool dude. I love watching you with others—friends, teammates, and cousins. You know what to say. You know how to make others feel good about themselves.

Your smile is amazing. You have a talent for connecting with others—reaching out and making them a part of your friendship circle.

I am so glad that I am one of your way older friends. Thank you for always greeting me with a hug. Your hugs make me feel so good.

I am looking forward to this summer. I want to be truly helpful to you in learning how to spell better. We will also do some other really great things—maybe even a little tennis if my ankle gets better.

Love you lots! Oh, HAPPY BIRTHDAY!

Grandpa Winn

include recognition for past successes in school, athletics, or other parts of their lives. Sometimes they provide counsel or encouragement for specific growth-related activities. Often the central themes of these letters are expressions of love and gratitude for the good people they are becoming. And obviously, we wish them a very happy birthday. Our birthday letters also contain a relatively small amount of cash.

I love receiving my yearly birthday letter. My grand-parents take notes on my life and my whereabouts. It is really lovely to receive some tips at my age so I can be successful. They also point out my successes within that year. It is always nice to know what you are doing right.

Maggie, Granddaughter, 19

By the way, these letters need not be preceded with a dinner. Grandchildren who live great distances from you will profit significantly from personally crafted birthday letters touting their achievements, expressing your advice, and conveying your love. Another benefit of these letters is they can be read and reread over time. Grandchildren can revisit the content of these letters months or years later, repeatedly enjoying the positive feelings experienced and reviewing any advice given.

Targeted but Informal Texting. Another means we use to connect and communicate with our grandkids is texting (see chapters 3 and 8). Texting is our primary way of staying in touch with our grandchildren and their parents. We use almost any excuse to connect with them. We frequently highlight achievements or accomplishments with these media sources because of the ease with which we can take and include photos and videos.

We are particularly responsive to the things we hear from our grandchildren's parents. If they share positive comments about a grandchild's spontaneous and unsolicited help in performing a challenging task like cleaning up a messy kitchen or organizing a garage, we immediately convey our delight and exuberance for freely given acts of service. These texts might read something like this: "Esther and Tanette, thank you so much for taking the time to surprise your mother with a completely clean and fully organized pantry. Doing worthwhile things without being asked says a lot about your maturity and commitment to generosity. Sending much, much love your way!"

Crazy-Fun/Informative Postcards. Another very well-received practice is sending postcards when we travel as a couple or as individuals (see chapter 5). Before the trip, we create address labels with each grandchild's name and home address. At different points in time during the journey, we take a few minutes to select attractive or educational postcards that match our grandchildren's emerging interests and

needs. We simply adhere the address labels to the selected cards. We then pen questions that require them to think about the featured individual(s), location, painting, setting, or whatever else is on the postcard, adjusting the questions and comments to each grandchild's age and capacities.

When we return home, we ask them about their post-cards and see what they have learned or remembered. These postcards give them a feel for various parts of our world and the people that make it unique and exceptional. They also communicate our desire to stay connected with them. Finally, they are a powerful means of expressing our love for them. Every child loves to receive something in the mail created specifically for him or her.

Our grandkids love and collect these cards. We encourage them to share these cards and their messages with their parents and friends.

> What I do remember and could talk about for days on end are the intentional grandparenting events that have changed my life and made me feel happy and fulfilled. My grandparents' genuine interest in Harry Potter and taking me to Barnes and Noble to pick up new books at midnight so we could dig into them; their kind, specific and observant letters, and postcards; and their penchant for using their time with me in meaningful ways is what I will always remember. The point here is mostly that, in pursuit of being a "killer" grandparent, you will prob-ably—no, definitely—goof up. But the highs will be so much higher than the lows. When your grandkids age and become more keen and astute, they'll realize that just as much as the successful pursuits, the hiccups and flops are massive demonstrations of love.
>
> *Noah, Grandson, 23*

Flops and Disasters. In the spirit of openness, we have had a few flops and disasters when it comes to grandparent-sponsored events. ⚡ One such event was a cousin party. We thought it would be fun to have our grandkids invite all their same-age cousins from the other side of each of their respective families to a party. This party was targeted at high school and college-age cousins. We thought we could establish a means for broadening friendships among and between cousins from different families.

We found a great location with a large outdoor area where we could play interactive games. We prepared three-foot hoagie sandwiches, fresh fruits, chips, punch, and cookies for the event. We thought we were set for success, but the party was mostly a bust. The activities we had chosen were totally off the mark. We knew almost instantly that our grandkids were unimpressed with the kind of games we had chosen. The only winner was the food.

Our grandkids still joke about the event. They often sarcastically say something like, "Grandpa, maybe we should have another cousin party—it was *so* much fun."

The big takeaway from this party was this: Don't make assumptions about what your grandkids want and enjoy. If you really want to plan an event for them, involve them in the planning and engage them in selecting the party's games and activities.

The cousin party wasn't our only flop. One of our most significant disasters occurred with our very first grandchild, Ben. Truthfully, Linda had nothing to do with this grave error in judgment. I was the culprit. As I revisit this experience, I am happy that I am still alive, given the magnitude of this mistake.

I don't remember precisely how old Ben, our grandson, was, but he was at a point in his life where he questioned the reality of Santa Claus. Without any concern for his parents and their potentially strong feelings, I thought he was ready for the truth. So, in a moment of stupidity and foolishness, I shared with him Santa's real identity. Of course, I encouraged him to keep this information to himself. I did not want him to damage the beliefs of his younger sisters regarding Santa. In short order, he shared his new insights with his mother. She was quite upset but over time kindly forgave me.

What follows is Ben's actual description of this disaster—now many years later:

> As a young child, there was someone I always knew I could trust, my Grandpa Winn. Seeing that I could trust him implicitly, I proceeded to ask him, "Grandpa, you would never lie to me, right?" He responded, "I will always tell you the truth."
>
> I immediately proceeded to ask the question, "Grandpa is Santa Claus real?" I put my grandpa in a very untenable position. Most grandparents would've lied, which wouldn't have been a bad thing. Grandpa Winn didn't lie. He answered the question and explained to me Santa Claus wasn't real. He did not share this information with my mom. Let's just say she was on fire about his actions for some time. This could seem very inconsequential, but this set a precedent. I know I will always be able to confide in my grandpa and receive the truth as he understands it.
>
> *Benjamin, Grandson, 28*

Focused Themes. Each year, we select a family theme—a focus for the year (see chapter 7). It is a way of drawing attention to behaviors or character traits that are important to us as grandparents. It is a way of showing our grandchildren what we really think is valuable and essential.

One such theme was *Manners Matter!* We wanted our grandchildren to be aware of and practiced in being polite and gracious—not only in their homes, but also in other settings, including school classrooms, restaurants, and other public and private spaces. Generally, we introduce these themes at the beginning of each year in conjunction with a family dinner.

We also have our grandchildren paint colorful, decorative wood blocks to which we adhere vinyl letters spelling out the specific theme—Manners Matter. We then encourage each family to put their block in a prominent place within their home to help them remember and focus on the behaviors associated with each year's theme. Throughout the year, we devote regular time to talking about the theme and how it is being embraced in their lives.

Informed Advocacy. Sometimes you can serve as advocates for your grandkids (see chapter 2). However, to do this well, you must be sure that your observations are accurate and warranted.

🔆 Some years ago, I met weekly with a grandson. He was a senior in high school and about a year older than his same-grade friends. During these early-morning sessions, we discussed various topics, including compassion, grace, justice, faith, and mercy. The purposes of these sessions varied. They were primarily devoted to understanding what it meant to be a good person, a caring friend.

On one of these mornings, he spoke at length about his ongoing interactions with his parents. Here is his story—now many years later.

As a young teenager, I loved to take dips in the pool of arrogance. Heck, I still do it on occasion. This arrogance caused me to argue with my parents about most everything. It didn't help that I was their first child, so it was literally their "first rodeo."

I was always frustrated that almost all of my close friends had more privileges than I did. It drove me absolutely nuts. It especially drove me nuts to see my friends making bad decisions and still having more rights and privileges. It just didn't seem fair. I always asked my parents for more leeway, and 97% of the time, I was met with a brick wall.

The frustration mounted until it led me to have a big, knockdown, drag-out discussion; I mean, a fight with my parents. I was so mad. I was doing all the right things. I was completing my home chores, doing well in school, and generally being a good person. But they wouldn't budge. I was so frustrated I drove to my grandpa's house and explained to him how I was feeling. I explained how I was doing all the right things (keeping a job, mostly completing my homework, etc.). I was not doing any bad things (getting poor grades, doing drugs, etc.).

I just wanted some answers to what I was doing wrong. This is the type of conversation that grandkids rarely have with their grandparents. I knew I could trust my grandpa, and I knew he would find a way to support me or help me see something I was missing. The conversation with him made me feel a lot better.

After this lively chat with Grandpa Winn, I wondered what steps I would now need to take. It was nice to get a few things off my chest and to share how I was feeling. I wondered if I would have to resume my discussion with my parents. Honestly, I really didn't want to talk to them again about my issues.

Grandpa Winn didn't tell me what he was going to do. The next day my parents told me they wanted to have a meeting with me. I was amazed by this announcement. During this meeting, they gave me a lot of leeway in running my life. It seemed to come from nowhere. I was so confused until they told me that my grandpa had called and talked to them last night. He advocated for me and suggested they meet me in the middle. I was so grateful to him. His decision to trust me and his willingness to talk to my parents dramatically impacted the relationship I had with them. It might have even saved our relationship. I will never forget that.

Benjamin, Grandson, 28

Vital Elements of *Grandparenting on Purpose*

What follows are some of the essential elements that describe the calling and work of grandparents. As you process each of these elements, think about where you are and how you could become more purposeful and intentional in your work and calling as a grandparent.

Authenticity in Expressing Love. Most young people are excellent detectors of insincerity and deception in adults. Because you are reading this book, we know your motivation is high and authentic. You genuinely want to support your grandkids in realizing their dreams and aspirations. You want to nurture them and help them become happy, caring, and responsible adults. Let's look at some ways you can do that.

As you know, sincere love can be expressed in many ways. It is complimenting others, paying attention to personal growth and change, showing genuine and welcomed affection (hugs and kisses), spending meaningful time with grandchildren, and providing regular doses of unhurried and active listening.

Sometimes, love is forgiving and showing compassion when grandkids have made mistakes. Working with them is also a remarkable way of showing love. Furthermore, they want to have fun with you. Often this comes in the form of playing games—even games with which they are unfamiliar, like jacks, kick the can and steal the flag—games you played as a child or youth.

The following are examples of expressions we use to show love, to affirm talents, and to support our grandchildren.

Rosemary (age twelve), how did you learn to swim so well? Are you preparing for a future in the Olympics?

Davidson (age eleven), we are amazed at your capacity to juke kids trying to tackle you in football games. Your skills are unbelievable. You are a natural athlete.

Jane (age fourteen), your skill in singing and playing the guitar has grown so much. We love hearing you make music. Your confidence in performing is so much better than it was just a short time ago.

Livie (age fourteen), we just heard you won the soccer game in the last minutes of the second half. Also, we understand you took the winning shot close to the mid-line of the field. Congratulations!

Gabe (age fifteen), at your recent concert, we were astounded with the quality of your performance. You seem to be naturally talented when it comes to playing the trombone.

Matt (age fifteen), you make us laugh so much. Your wit and joke-telling are incredible! We sometimes laugh at things you say when we shouldn't. That's because they are so funny and original.

Dane (age fifteen), you have a real talent for developing novel, crazy-funny words like "egantistical." You also have a lot of creative horsepower.

Rebekah (age eighteen), your anti-bullying campaign was incredible. Thank you for having the courage to tackle a real problem in your school and elsewhere. We are immensely proud of your efforts and novel approaches to addressing this serious issue in your school and community.

Tanette (age eighteen), you are Miss Persistent! Thanks for not giving up on yourself. Passing the admission exam for your dental assistant program was a real achievement. With this kind of courage, there is no end to what you can accomplish.

Sam (age eighteen), we recently discovered that you, without any incentives or demands, helped your mother with some major housework. She had no idea that you had taken on this cleaning challenge. When she arrived home, she was thrilled with what you had done to make an otherwise cluttered kitchen clean and neat. You are amazing.

Abby (age twenty), where did you learn to be so organized? Thank you so much for helping us sort through all the equipment and tools in our garage. Also, thank you for being so positive as you directed our efforts.

These affirmative statements help your grandkids discover who they are, what they might be good at, and who they might become. They also contribute to the quality of the relationships you wish to establish and sustain with each of them.

Use your own language style to convey your support and delight for your grandkids. The critical ingredient for your expressions is that they are genuine.

Benefits of Love Well Expressed. When love is genuinely expressed, it soothes and supports grandchildren in powerful ways. It often helps them persist in doing and completing personally challenging tasks. It makes the receiving of counsel and advice from you more comfortable and potentially more acceptable. It makes discipline more productive when they need to be corrected or encouraged to behave in more appropriate and responsible ways. It adds strength to their resolve when they are attempting something new and challenging. It lets them know that they are not alone. Authentic love works its charm in many ways.

Love is at the heart of everything you do as a grandparent. Your grandchildren will sense this love and thrive on it. It will sustain them when they are struggling with problems. It will uplift them when they are sad, perplexed, or burdened. Your love amplifies the support and care provided by their parents. In reality, your grandchildren can never experience too much love.

As affirmed earlier, your grandchildren will know if the love you express is authentic. This love might be expressed as an unexpected visit; a batch of newly baked oatmeal-chocolate-chip cookies; unanticipated attendance at a sporting event, recital, play, or other similar activities; a carefully crafted, unexpected letter; a supportive text delivering some encouragement; or an unscheduled, quick visit bringing a grandchild's favorite treat or food.

Love is shown in endless ways by grandparents. However, to do it well, you must know your grandchildren well—their strengths, interests, challenges, and aspirations. You must know what they are doing. You must know what they are passionate about and what they like and love (see chapter 2).

Inspiration Seekers. At the outset of this particular section, we want to be clear about our intent. It is not to favor or recommend a specific faith or religion. Our purpose is to share with you our beliefs about inspiration, its sources, and its impacts. You, of course, will determine what to take seriously and what to ignore.

From our perspective, inspiration is a divine form of help and assistance in framing and addressing real-life, challenging problems. It is a profound form of direction and insight. Inspiration is also a matchless form of spiritual light that gives clarity and definition to perplexing issues and their resolution.

We believe all grandparents have the right to inspiration in their sacred calling and work (see chapter 8). In our family, Linda was particularly adept at receiving guidance and inspiration for our work and calling as grandparents. She was remarkably proficient in her capacity to ponder, seek divine assistance, and come up with valuable ideas for addressing family challenges and helping with grandchild-specific problems.

Inspiration comes to us in various forms. It may be strong intuitions or impressions. It may come through conversations and feelings we receive while seeking advice from others. It may come from serious pondering. It may come from sacred readings, meditation, or prayer. It may come through caring friends or professionals.

You will know or discover what works best for you. Use inspiration to find ways to support and guide your grandchildren and their parents.

🔆 The following simple example may be useful to you. When two of our daughters were in high school, we were concerned about how they were moving through their teenage years. Linda began to think about what we could do to give them some experiences that would positively broaden their perspectives and strengthen their positive perceptions of themselves and others. She came up with a brilliant idea. She called several mothers of their peers to see if they would be interested in supporting the creation of a singing group. This group would receive vocal lessons at the home of a talented, young, very competent mother. There was immediate buy-in.

For the better part of one year, our daughters and their peers met weekly with this mother to receive vocal instruction and to learn songs they could perform. In addition to her teaching, this young mother provided a lot of excellent modeling about being a woman, a mother, and a wife. Our two daughters thoroughly enjoyed the experience. Moreover, the sociality that accompanied each lesson and several performances contributed significantly to their positive feelings about themselves and others in the group.

Again, we believe that divine help is available to you. Actively seek it. Respond to the inspiration you receive. We believe it will be tailored to your particular circumstances and needs.

What Do You Want for Your Grandchildren?

We suspect your wishes and wants for your grandchildren, and their parents are similar to ours. You want the best for them during each phase of their lives. You want to be helpful to them in responsible ways. You want to support them in realizing worthwhile goals. You want to sustain them in developing and using their talents and capabilities. You want them to become the parents, neighbors, friends, and associates that families, communities, and workplaces so desperately need—individuals who are other-centered, caring, responsible, and full of integrity.

What Makes a Difference?

For a moment, let's talk about practices that reliably make a difference in all children's lives. First, we know that having at least one significant, supportive adult in your life makes a tremendous difference in your happiness as a child, youth, or young adult. In many cases, these supporting adults are school volunteers, counselors, tutors, coaches, teachers, or you!

What makes these individuals so useful and effective is their capacity to form and nurture caring relationships. They know how to listen well. They know how to provide feedback that will be received positively and put into action. They know how to encourage and support others in their aspirations and deepest desires. They understand the importance of affirming and sustaining others in their talent development. They not only take an interest in others, but they maintain this interest over time. They are there for important events. They are there at times of uncertainty and pain. Candidly, they know how powerful love is and how it is made real in young people's lives.

Frankly, these are the same behaviors that will make a difference in your grandchildren's lives. Take a moment now to consider your current strengths and how you could improve. Again, have a growth mentality. Target one behavior for change; you might choose to be a better listener, to praising more frequently, to be less judgmental, or to be silent more regularly. You can grow, change, and flourish as a grandparent.

💡 As you know, Linda had Grandma Rhoda, who was consistently there for her during her middle school, high school, and young adult years. She lived very quietly and humbly in a small basement apartment of Linda's home. When Linda arrived home from school each day, her grandmother was there with a treat and a listening ear.

Linda's Grandma Rhoda made an enormous difference in her life. She was a caring listener and a trustworthy confidant. Linda knew she could share her troubles and concerns as well as her triumphs with her grandmother.

Grandma Rhoda's most meaningful gifts to her granddaughter Linda were her time, thoughtful listening, and sincere friendship. Just as Rhoda did, you can make a difference in your grandchildren's lives regardless of your relative wealth, educational background, upbringing, marital status, or other factors.

We believe that small, repetitive, spontaneous, and loving actions of grandparents can meet and do meet some of the most profound needs of grandchildren and their parents. These actions may include a daily conversation, a regular letter or text, hurry-free listening, a personalized treat, or a card—whatever you are inspired and prompted to do. Again, these little but significant actions don't depend on your income level, education, or social status. They don't depend on how far away you live. They mainly require your time and a consistent commitment to simple acts of love, kindness, listening, and affirmation.

No Two Are the Same

We know that no two grandparents are the same. Some grandparents are the full-time parents of their grandkids. Some have a lot of resources; others have few. Some live great distances from their grandchildren, thus lessening the opportunities to be with them. Some grandparents are insulted by their own children and have little or no access to their grandkids. Some grandparents are treated with hostility and contempt by their children's spouses. Other grandparents serve without the benefit or support of a partner because of divorce, death, disability, or other factors. Chapter 4 presents several ideas for addressing challenging relationships that you may be experiencing with your children and their spouses.

All Families Have Special Needs

Extended families come in all hues, shapes, and sizes. They also present different opportunities as well as challenges for grandparents. Virtually every grandparent will encounter grandchildren with disabilities, health issues, and other related conditions. Similarly, many grandparents nurture and support children who are single parents, who are LGBTQ+, who are remarried, who have spouses who are absent for significant periods serving in the military or other occupations, or who live thousands of miles away—to mention only a few. Also, grandparents may have grandchildren who are foster children, stepchildren, or who are adopted like five of our grandchildren. Some grandparents are the legal guardians of their grandchildren.

Given this diversity between families, we want to be sensitive to what you might be experiencing as a grandparent. We do not want to ignore the obvious—every family is different. Nonetheless, as you come to understand and faithfully use the fundamental principles of *Grandparenting on Purpose*, we are confident that you will begin to see positive results in your grandchildren and their parents. It may take some time—even considerable effort to achieve the outcomes you desperately desire.

As indicated earlier, not everything we share will apply to you. That would be impossible. However, we are committed to sharing what we believe to be our very best work, ideas, and practices.

Our heartfelt desire is to share our best attempts to be the most responsible and caring grandparents we could be. You will be the best judge as to what activities, practices, and ideas should be considered and put in motion in your family. Here is your opportunity to pick and choose methods and practices that make sense to you.

What Will It Take for You to Become More Purposeful?

Many of you are naturally inclined to be purposeful in your calling and work as grandparents. You are deliberate in your actions and clear-cut in your aspirations and aims. If this is the case, congratulations! You have already experienced many of the joys and benefits of being connected with your grandchildren. As you move through this book, you will be adding to your store of valuable routines, practices, and activities.

If you are less purposeful in your present actions as a grandparent, begin with small steps. Simply try one or two of the ideas that speak to you and see what happens. Gradually expand your efforts.

As you know, so many of our behaviors and aspirations are rooted in our experiences with our parents and grandparents. This is your opportunity to develop new ways of thinking and behaving as a grandparent. This is your chance to start anew.

The good news is this. The ideas and practices we share with you are relatively easy to understand. Simply ignore those ideas or methods that don't speak to you. With commitment, practice, and effort, you can grow as a grandparent, gradually becoming the kind of grandparent you wish to be.

Moving through the Book: A Quick Overview

Now you are ready to move on, discovering ideas and practices that will help you connect with and build great relationships with your grandchildren and their parents. Take a moment now to determine where you want to jump in.

Here is a quick overview of what you can anticipate. Chapter 2 speaks to ideas about connecting with your grandchildren and their parents. It centers on determining their needs. What do they like? What are their favorite activities? It also reveals many ways to discover their needs. You will find ways to connect with those who live near or far away from you. Knowing your grandchildren's needs is essential to your success in connecting and building relationships with them.

Chapter 3 details the steps you can take to communicate with grandchildren at a distance and those who live close to you. This chapter provides concrete and simple ideas for developing and maintaining positive relationships with your grandchildren—practices that deepen and cement family bonds and connections.

Chapter 4 provides precise information on mending relationships, developing plans for reconciliation, and moving forward with relationship-building efforts. This chapter emerged as we obtained critical reviews from dear friends and knowledgeable professionals. If you are struggling in establishing relationships with some of your children and their spouses, this chapter is written for you!

Chapter 5 reveals the purpose and effects of powerful family traditions. Moreover, we share our best and most popular family traditions with you. Each tradition has withstood the test of time. Our grandkids thoroughly love and anticipate these traditions each year as a part of holidays or other regular family activities. Use this chapter as a springboard for identifying and launching new traditions in your family. Look for ideas and practices that speak to you.

Family routines are the focus of chapter 6. Family routines and practices are smaller versions of traditions. Again, we present our routines, hoping that they will spawn some new thoughts and ideas for your family. Don't miss what we consider to be our most significant routine. Let's see if it becomes your most important family routine or practice too.

Chapter 7 presents our attempts to develop highly functional and beneficial behaviors by launching annual family themes. As you will see, we have focused on actions related to generosity, working hard, and being kind.

If you are interested in building and fostering spirituality in grandchildren, chapter 8 reveals our attempts to help our grandchildren develop attributes associated with spirituality. We begin the chapter with several questions about spirituality, explaining what the concept means to us. We then share our efforts to nurture it in our grandchildren.

Chapter 9 revisits many of the concepts and principles we have talked about in previous chapters. It addresses the question, *What do grandchildren want and need from their grandparents?* We take a serious stab at answering this question.

Lastly, chapter 10 provides a wrap-up, a restatement of important concepts directly related to being the grandparent you wish to be. It ends with an invitation to continue your involvement with us as a caring and concerned grandparent at grandparentingonpurpose.com.

As you move through the various chapters of the book, look for ideas and actions that make sense to you. Don't get bogged down with comparisons or judgments about your past or current grandparenting practices. Remember, your purpose is to grow, to discover, and to develop as a grandparent. Also, remember that each of us comes to the grandparenting enterprise with very different experiences and dispositions. Have fun! Say to yourself, *"Those Egans are totally over the top, but they are well-intentioned. I will look for ideas and practices that fit me and make sense for my family."*

What are the key elements of *Grandparenting on Purpose*, as you understand them?

_____

_____

_____

_____

_____

_____

_____

_____

_____

_____

_____

As you consider these elements, where are you most interested in growing and changing?

_____

_____

_____

_____

_____

_____

_____

_____

_____

_____

What ideas or practices presented in this chapter resonate with you? What are the springboard ideas for your family?

_____

_____

_____

_____

_____

_____

_____

_____

_____

_____

_____

What do you most need to do right now to motivate and support your learning and growing in becoming a more purposeful grandparent?

_____

_____

_____

_____

_____

_____

_____

_____

_____

Chapter 2

Discovering the Needs of Your Grandchildren and Their Parents

Grandparents should spend time with their children and grandchildren. They need to uplift and teach. They should teach about their past, their faith, and anything that comes to them. They need to know their grandchildren, their needs, wants, and passions.

Livie, Granddaughter, 14

Getting to Know Your Grandchildren Well

How much do you know about your grandchildren? Are you familiar with their needs, struggles, strivings, and aspirations? Also, are you aware of the needs of your married children and their spouses? Take a minute or two to think about each of your grandchildren. What do you know about them? What do you understand about them? Are you familiar with their talents, interests, desires, and challenges? Think about what new and supportive things you have done or could do to be more responsive to their needs—small, medium, or large.

It's virtually impossible to respond to anyone's needs unless you clearly understand what they are. The same is true of your children and their spouses. Be observant. Be an unhurried listener. Come to understand your family members well so you can support them in becoming happy and healthy people.

Purposeful grandparents are experts in discerning their grandchildren's needs. Knowing all their needs is not appropriate. We are confident that you will be wise in determining what your proper role is and what boundaries you should honor in determining needs. Once you understand your grandchildren's needs, you can take steps to be responsive to them—if you can be genuinely helpful. The operative phrase is this: *If you can be genuinely useful.* Don't intrude in areas where you might be seen as a meddler or troublemaker.

Stating the obvious, grandparents don't respond to needs that enable "bad" or unhealthy behaviors. As a grandparent, you need to empower your grandchildren in positive, healthy, and responsible ways. Ask yourself this question: "What is the responsible thing to do?" You need to be a positive enabler.

You thoughtfully respond to needs that give rise to resilience, personal identity, spirituality, responsibility, kindness, courage, integrity, independence, trustworthiness, and other positive traits—some of the most essential elements of real character. Moreover, you take specific steps to sustain your grandchildren in becoming contributing and caring adults.

WELE Lunches. We want to share an example of how we attempt to be attentive and responsive to our children and their spouses. We have sponsored our WELE lunches (Winn Egan/Linda Egan lunches) for several years. These lunches

are small, informal gatherings. We are fortunate to live relatively close to each other. We can quickly get together for
these lunches.

During the school year, we host these lunches at our home
or at a nearby restaurant. Our daughters and daughter-
in-law are usually the ones who attend these gatherings.
Sometimes our son or sons-in-law participate. Sometimes,
one or several of our older, college-age grandchildren also
come. Sometimes only one can come for lunch. When this
is the case, we use this precious, one-on-one time to explore
what is happening in that particular family.

We schedule these WELE get-
togethers during the noon
hour. These lunches
mostly occur in the
quiet of our home.
Our cuisine is simple.
One of our favor-
ite menu items is a
cheeseburger salad
(a green salad with a
huge cheeseburger placed
on top of it without a bun).

The best parts of these lunches are the conversations.
These free-flowing discussions give us a chance to learn
about what is taking place in each family. It's a time to hear
and discuss whatever surfaces during these times together.

We often talk about past or upcoming family events, athletic games, and school-related performances—anything
and everything that might provide avenues for deepening
relationships, supporting talent development, helping each

other make sense of child- or family-related issues, and providing encouragement for personal growth.

The WELE lunches also give us opportunities to ask our children questions such as these: What are your concerns right now? What is happening to Ben? What is the latest with Skyler's work? How is Maggie responding to her apprenticeship? What can we do to be helpful? However, most of the time, we just listen and see what is happening in each family.

These are not interrogation lunches! They are times for sharing and discovering how we might be useful to our grandchildren and their parents. If a more personal approach to a potential concern is needed, we follow up with an individual visit or phone call.

These lunches are not something you need to do. We share this idea with you in hopes that it will serve as a springboard for you in creating beneficial ways to discover and respond to the needs of your grandchildren and their parents. We suggest you develop something like these lunches to communicate with your adult children and their spouses.

If you have nurtured excellent relationships with your children's spouses, they will also benefit from informal conversations and connections with you. As you have these conversations, listen carefully. Be willing to listen a little longer and to convey your genuine concern and love. Once you have a good feel for what needs to be done, respond with sensitivity and respect.

For children and their spouses who live great distances from your home, consider using other means you will discover as you move through this chapter. Also, be innovative and creative; maybe a little tweaking of a recommended practice or idea will work for you and your family.

Reliable Sources of Information about Your Grandchildren's Needs. The best and most reliable information about your grandchildren's needs most often comes from their parents— your children and their spouses. Of course, your relationship with them needs to be such that they feel comfortable sharing this information with you. Likewise, their willingness to share information about their children is enhanced if you have regular opportunities for natural and relaxed conversations with them.

We realize that many grandparents face significant challenges in interacting with their married children and their spouses. For this reason, we have devoted an entire chapter to these challenges (see chapter 4). We have attempted to provide some valuable suggestions for determining what potential steps you could take and how you might proceed in repairing a damaged or nonexistent relationship.

Check-In Calls. Regular check-in or how-are-you-doing phone calls also serve us well. This is an easy way of connecting with our children and grandchildren who live great distances from our home. In making these periodic calls, we are careful to be sure that our timing is right. Also, we often receive what-do-you-think-we-ought-to-do calls from the parents and even sometimes from our grandchildren. The motivations for these calls vary, but at their heart, these calls come because our children and grandkids trust us. They know we will keep confidential any information they share with us. Generally, these calls center on some persistent behavior issues such as anxiety, depressed mood, or unexpected aggression. Or they may relate to concerns such as this one: "Do you have any creative ideas for asking a girl for a high school dance?"

💡 In one family's case, the issue was persistent lying. The questions posed by the mother of this grandchild were these: "What do I do? How should I respond? Is there something I am doing that rewards this behavior? I'm frightened about my child's future if this behavior continues. My husband and I need some help. What do you think we should do?"

Our first response is to listen and to learn as much as we can about the identified behavior and/or problem. We also try to assess how much the individual or parents want us to be involved. Are they just sharing information? Do they really want us to do something? Often, just freely talking about an issue or problem is sufficient and helpful.

It is perfectly all right to ask these kinds of questions: "How could we be most helpful to you?" Or "What would you most like us to do to be useful to you and your family?"

After we have a clear sense of how they want us to be involved, we may ask them. How often does this behavior happen? Are there any recent events that have encouraged or supported the behavior? When does it most often occur? What seems to trigger it? What is your usual response to it? We also attempt to get a feel for what she was feeling. Moreover, we try to determine what she and her husband had done to address the lying. What, if any, help had they sought?

Obviously, if we feel confident in providing some helpful advice, we give it immediately. However, we usually tell the parents we will get back in touch with them as soon as possible, assuring them that we will do our best to inform ourselves.

Then we do all we can to educate ourselves and seek meaningful solutions for the identified problem. If we cannot be useful immediately, we try to communicate our intent to be helpful. Frequently, before we conclude the conversation, we ask, "Is there is anything else that you want to share—something you may have missed?" This kind of question opens the door for something that may need to have been said but did not surface during the beginning of our conversation.

Fortunately, we found beneficial, parent-centered materials from trusted sources that answered many of the mother's concerns regarding the causes, seriousness, and treatment of lying. As soon as we found these materials, we made them immediately available to her. Within several months, the lying behavior seemed to remediate itself. The child's mother moved on to the next opportunities and challenges of her children.

In some instances, support groups are available for parents and other caregivers. These groups are often sponsored by advocacy groups—groups of parents and professionals who have had a lot of experience with a given disability, addiction, or health condition. We have a granddaughter with Type 1 diabetes. We benefitted immensely from the Juvenile Diabetes Research Foundation and its family support and advocacy groups.

The point is this: You want to be seen as a valuable and committed resource for your children. They know that when they seek help and support, they can come to you even if you are only able to listen and provide some emotional first aid.

As we make check-in calls, we are frequently prompted to ask specific questions about a particular grandchild about whom we have concerns. Or we ask about each grandchild individually. Then we listen thoroughly, sincerely attempting to understand what is being said and what needs and emotions are being shared.

Sometimes, we actively explore or suggest ways in which we might be helpful. Would some time away from home be useful. Would that child like to spend time at our house? Maybe we could bring you some dinner or have you come for dinner? Would some help with carpooling make a difference? Could we help by taking one or several of your children with us to a movie? If we are feeling exceedingly competent, we might even offer to help with homework or a science fair project.

Be Alert. We often learn a lot by merely being very sensitive to what we see and hear at family-related events. Sometimes, silence tells us a lot about what is happening in a particular family or with a specific grandchild. We look for signs of sadness, disengagement, or weariness. When we observe signs of distress or discomfort, we brainstorm as a couple things we might do and genuinely want to do to be helpful. Then we offer our ideas for helping and determine if they are acceptable.

Determine Their Needs. Set aside some appropriate time to think about each of your grandchildren individually. If your spouse is willing and available, brainstorm together what you think each grandchild needs. Start with the grandchild you consider to be the most burdened or needy. Or start with a grandchild who is not so needy, freeing up parents to devote their energies to the child who most needs their support. The point is this: be helpful where you believe you can make authentic and valuable contributions and a difference.

For purposes of discussion, let's assume the first grandchild of concern is a granddaughter. Given your relationship with this granddaughter, how could you improve it? How could you make it better, more durable? Maybe a good or excellent relationship already exists with her. If so, you are well on your way to being helpful to her, her parents, and her family.

Carefully list the needs of your granddaughter as you see them. Does she need support for school-related tasks? Does she have close and caring friends? How are her parents handling her challenges and opportunities? Does she have good outlets for expressing herself, demonstrating her emerging talents, and letting off steam? Does she have opportunities to do hard things that build personal resilience and character? If you can answer these and similar questions, you are well on your way to determining what you might do to be helpful.

If your personal connection with this granddaughter is less than desirable, identify potential steps to improve your relationship. Then put your plan in action.

Learn the Answers to These Questions

Assuming you have a good relationship with this granddaughter and have her trust, do you know the answers to these questions?

- What are her capacities?
- What are her strengths?
- What are her passions?
- What are her challenges?
- What are her aspirations?
- What does she enjoy doing with you?

- Who are her closest friends?
- Who are the other adults in her life that she connects with and enjoys—her parents, a coach, a teacher, or a youth leader?
- What foods does she love?
- What music does she like?
- What, if anything, does she like about school?
- What is just one thing you could do to bring some joy into her life?

Knowing the answers to these and related questions informs the steps you might take to help her. Then in concert with your granddaughter's parents, determine specific actions you could put in place. Incrementally, put your plan into action. Remember, you may need to make periodic adjustments—adapting to what you see and experience in trying to bring success to your granddaughter and her parents.

Be Advocates. Advocating for a grandchild can be tricky. We spoke about advocacy in chapter 1. To advocate effectively for a grandchild, you must have a trusting relationship with his or her parents. They must sense that you are not attempting to manipulate them—that you are genuinely sincere and confident in your advocacy recommendations. You must also be sure that your advocacy is supported with appropriate observations and justifications.

Putting Yourself in a Position to Make a Difference. Knowing your grandchildren's authentic needs places you in a position to act and be helpful to them and their parents. As you actively respond and meet their needs in healthy ways, you demonstrate your love for them. You fundamentally show them what it means to be an involved and committed grandparent.

Grandparent-to-Grandparent Chats. We have found that regular conversations and reviews related to each of our grandchildren are invaluable. During an evening meal or at some other appropriate time, we discuss each grandchild. These timely chats help us remain focused, current, and centered on what matters most—the health and happiness of all family members. As we discuss each grandchild, we keep in mind what we have observed over the past few months. We test our impressions and observations to see if we agree on what we are seeing. We brainstorm things we might do to be helpful. We then commit to some immediate and appropriate actions.

Start Now

One by one, write the names of your grandchildren on separate sheets of paper. Following each of their names, list the
things you know about each of them. As prompted, identify
what you believe to be three of their current, most essential
needs. For example, you might write this about one of your
granddaughters:

> Jill is unsure of herself in social situations. She has a hard
> time relating to or speaking informally with others—
> even her cousins. She also seems to struggle with form-
> ing friendships with others. She excels academically but
> appears to derive little enjoyment from her schoolwork.
> She likes music and might benefit from learning to play
> an instrument, such as a guitar or ukulele.

Once you have identified your grandchildren's needs,
you are better able to provide support to them and their parents. Responding appropriately to grandchildren's needs
is a gratifying and fulfilling activity for us. The smiles, the
hugs, and the expressions of appreciation that emanate from
our grandchildren in response to our attempts to be helpful

are priceless. Take some time now to determine the needs of your precious grandchildren. Then take some measured and inspired steps to implement your action plan.

We encourage you to be attentive and alert as you interact with your children and their spouses. Be especially vigilant during informal events or activities. Look for small signs of displeasure or disappointment. Also, look for signs of contentment, happiness, and success.

Use your observations to determine how your loved ones are doing and what they need. Based on what you see and feel, you can decide what steps need to be taken to support your grandchildren and their parents.

What are three or four things you have learned about determining your grandchildren's needs?

_____

_____

_____

_____

_____

_____

_____

_____

_____

_____

When you consider all your grandchildren and their parents, who most needs your love and concern now?

_____

_____

_____

_____

_____

_____

_____

_____

_____

What are their needs? What will you do immediately and over time?

_____

_____

_____

_____

_____

_____

_____

_____

_____

_____

Chapter 3

Connecting with Grandchildren

What makes a good grandparent? It's someone who goes out of their way to care about my cousins and me.

Dane, Grandson, 15

One-of-a-Kind, Personalized Support

Grandchildren benefit in significant ways when they are connected to their grandparents. As we affirmed earlier, you provide a one-of-a-kind, personalized support for your grandchildren and their families that can be significant. Your grandchildren need all the love they can get. You are one of the vital sources of this love if you have healthy and satisfying relationships with them.

Your support comes in many forms. As you know, the best kinds of support are tailored to your grandchildren's specific and unique needs. Knowing your grandchildren well makes it possible for you to deliver precise encouragement, feedback, and attention that is unrivaled and custom-made.

Your grandchildren may live some distance from you, even in other states or countries. When this is the case, you need to be more creative and inventive in regularly connecting with them. You might use apps such as Skype, Zoom, Google Duo, or Google Chat to communicate with them. We used several novel approaches while our children and their spouses lived or worked great distances from our home.

The Jacob Books. For years, we had several families who lived hundreds of miles away. In most instances, these families lived humbly because of the financial and other obligations associated with their schooling or entry-level employment.

One of these families resided in Indianapolis. Facebook, Instagram, and other social media had not yet been developed. We had to find creative ways to stay in touch with them and their children.

Our daughter Mary came up with a brilliant plan to stay connected with both sets of grandparents and their very young son, Jacob. It was a personalized, interactive book that chronicled his and their family's experiences during each month. It was replete with photographs, his emerging language, and other events of interest. It was a scrapbook of sorts.

Mary sent copies of the book through the mail to each set of grandparents. We, in turn, did the same. We also used photos and detailed commentary to capture the exciting things we were doing. We also attached pictures and

descriptions of our monthly activities to the emerging book. We loved receiving the book with each new grandson-centered chapter. We also know that he loved receiving our family chapters too.

The book became one of his most significant and prized treasures. It also became a permanent representation of cherished moments and activities that occurred in each family. It was a terrific way of staying connected, even though we were hundreds of miles away. Even today, this is one of his most valued keepsakes. His younger sister Maggie also benefitted from the creation of this kind of personalized book.

With the advent of social media, the kinds of information conveyed in the Jacob and Maggie Books can now be delivered on platforms such as Facebook, Instagram, and other applications. All these platforms negate the problems associated with distance and time. Moreover, the speed with which they can deliver engaging and compelling content is remarkable.

Timely and Targeted Texting. Almost all our older grandchildren have cell phones. They use them for everything.

It seems that they use their phones primarily and repeatedly for texting and real-time postings—hundreds of times a day. This is their chief means for communicating with their friends, parents, and us—their grandparents.

If you are not a skilled texter, you need to up your game! You need to become adept at communicating as your grandchildren do. If you are unskilled in texting, you will miss many, if not most opportunities to encourage and support your grandchildren. By the way, your grandchildren will be happy to share their skills with you—just ask them.

Currently, we use texting to stay connected with our grandchildren and their parents. We also make frequent use of an app called GroupMe. This app allows us to send texts to multiple grandchildren at the same time. We now have four family groups: a parent and grandparent group, a college-age / married couples group, an entire family group, and a grandchildren group. We use these groups almost daily. It is an excellent way of sending greetings, giving shout-outs, and announcing family events.

Just days ago, we announced the annual Thanksgiving Egan Turkey Bowl. We received immediate replies from most of our grandchildren, confirming their desire to participate in this yearly, family-wide, immensely fun tradition.

We use individual texting to congratulate grandchildren on noteworthy achievements or behaviors. Recently, one of our daughters told us how her son had gone out of his way to help their family. For several days, he had volunteered without any prompting to do things that were genuinely helpful to her. After hearing about this from his mother, we sent him a text conveying our delight at his freely given service to his mother and family. We believe he thoroughly enjoyed and benefitted from our acknowledgment of his contributions. We think this kind of support will encourage him to continue to be generous in responding to his family and friends' unique needs.

In like manner, we recently celebrated Thanksgiving at our daughter's home. She became ill just before the big day.

Her husband and children put together a fantastic feast. That night as we were about to retire, we sent each contributing grandchild a text expressing our appreciation for their efforts and contributions to a beautiful meal and celebration. Of course, we did the same with their dad, who prepared most of the delicious Thanksgiving dinner.

We believe these small gestures go a long way in building and sustaining relationships. They also help our grandchildren know how much we appreciate behaviors that represent generosity, kindness, and inclusion. Our grandchildren often reciprocate by sending us texts that convey their appreciation for our care and concern. We love these notes and the positive feelings they engender in us.

Don't miss even the smallest opportunities to support and sustain your grandchildren as they demonstrate generosity, kindness, and regard for others—especially as they show concern and compassion for their own family members. The cumulative power of these notes and texts is lasting and mighty. They can shape and influence your grandchildren in very positive ways.

Well-Timed Phone Calls and Even a Few Surprise Calls. We often use phone calls to connect with our grandchildren. These calls serve many purposes. Usually, they are booster shots that strengthen the power of messages delivered previously via texting. These calls often express gratitude for service rendered, acknowledge small and/or large achievements, or serve as a check-in to see how a grandchild is doing. We usually begin these calls with this statement: "I was thinking of you and thought I should give you a call."

Some calls are follow-ups to previously observed behaviors. For example, we discovered a granddaughter who was crying during a family party. We were not sure what had caused her sadness and discontent. We gave her a call to see if she felt better and if she wanted to talk about what had happened. Calls like these let your grandchildren know you care about how they are feeling and doing. They also convey a message that you want to be helpful. If you think a call might be soothing or useful to a grandchild, take some time today to contact them and let them know you are there for them.

Sometimes, we may feel that we have offended or hurt a grandchild with some action or ill-conceived comment. Generally, we begin these calls with something like this: "I just want to briefly talk to you. I hope I didn't hurt or offend you with my recent comments. If this is the case, I just wanted to say I'm so sorry. And I want to make things right." Then I listen to see how the grandchild responds to my request for understanding and forgiveness. These calls are often the most tender of all, as they usually give rise to painful feelings and strong emotions. The purpose of these calls is to repair hurt or damaged feelings and re-establish lost connections.

As mentioned earlier, spontaneous check-in calls are also useful in conveying love, concern, and interest. We love to receive calls from our grandchildren that begin with these words: "I had a few minutes, and I just wanted to say hi and see how you are doing." Your grandchildren will feel the same way. They love the notion that you are thinking about them and their well-being. Like you, they will be thrilled with your I-was-thinking-about-you calls.

Personal Letters. We know very few kids who don't like personal letters. Some letters or cards are expected. The kinds of messages we are talking about here are those that are unexpected—letters that come spontaneously from you, notes from the heart.

They are like the I-was-thinking-about-you-phone calls. Their central messages are these: "I think about you a lot. I felt prompted to send some love your way. I have included a little surprise for you and your friends."

Postcards. We talked about postcards in chapter 1. I used to travel a lot because of my job. In preparation for these post-card opportunities, I printed self-adhesive mailing labels with each grandchild's name and home address. I used these labels to make the mailing and posting process extremely simple.

When I selected the postcard for each grandchild, I considered his or her age and interests. In like manner, I individualized the commentary on each postcard—making sure that the postcard was totally suitable to each grandchild's needs and developmental level. Often I posed questions such as these: "Ask your parents where I am. Ask them what they know about this animal." Or "What do you know

about this person? Why is she so important to us and our country?"

> When I was nine, Grandpa Winn sent me a postcard with a group of Native American men wearing impressive feather headdresses. On the back of the card, Grandpa wrote, "Look at these amazing men! I wonder what they are thinking about? Love you lots! Gpa Winn" The men had serious faces and wrinkles. I thought about why they had wrinkles and what their lives were like. The postcard made me feel totally loved and remembered.
>
> *Elizabeth, Granddaughter, 23*

Our grandchildren have received cards from all parts of the United States and from several foreign countries. I know they loved collecting these cards, and I loved sending them. It was a distinctive approach of saying I think about you often. Again, having the labels readily available made it easy for me to send each grandchild a personal note or an engaging, age-appropriate question. I just purchased the postcards, penned quick notes, adhered stamps, and took them to the hotel desk.

Grandparent-Funded Dinners or Treats. Periodically, your grandkids and their parents benefit from a dinner sponsored and funded by you. It is the kind of surprise that the entire family loves. It gives them a chance to be together in a fun setting. It also offers parents a reprieve from the usual demands of dinner preparations.

These dinners also allow parents to teach well-established, restaurant- and etiquette-related skills, such as the placement and purpose of napkins, waiting in line, being polite, behaving well in public settings, and expressing appreciation for services rendered. These funded dinners need not be frequent—just often enough to make them unique and memorable.

You will know you are making a difference if your grandchildren text you and send you pictures and commentary about their away-from-home, family-friendly, grandparent-funded dinners.

Other equally fun, food-centered surprises may be providing a family's favorite dessert, candy, or other treats. The food or treats need not be expensive. It is the thought that counts and what the surprise represents—you and your love. Imagine your son or daughter saying this at the end of a customary evening dinner: "Your Grandpa Winn has provided a special dessert for tonight's meal. Let's see if you can guess what it is."

It is not the cost of the meal or treats; it is the surprise and what it represents. You may not be able to fund a family dinner, but we are confident you can surprise your grandchildren with a little treat. Surprises create their own magic!

Birthday Letters. As you learned in chapter 1, birthday letters are one of our favorite means for connecting with our grandchildren. Our grandchildren really treasure these

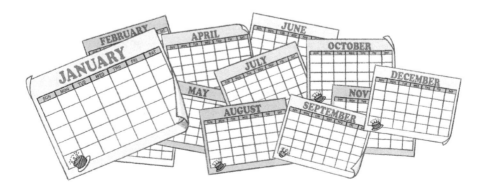

letters. When they receive them via the mail or monthly family birthday party/dinner, our grandchildren immediately read them. These letters are often more prized than customary gifts and presents. Moreover, they can be kept and cherished for years.

Birthday Letter to a Grandson

Dear _____,

We're so glad to be your grandparents. It is hard to believe that you're about to be eligible to drive a car. We're so thankful that you have been blessed with so many capacities. You're polite. You're smart. You're witty and intelligent. You're on the brink of beginning your first year of high school. A lot is coming at you, but with consistent effort and the support of your loving family, you will be able to reach your potential. You will be able to bless many lives.

    This may sound somewhat weird or be a little premature, but you're preparing to become a good man, a great husband, and a kind father. Watch your own dad, your uncles, and others whom you respect. Learn what it means to be a truly good man, husband, and father.

    As you become eligible to date, drive, and move toward greater independence, continue to build the trust of your parents and others. Trust takes months and years to establish. However, it can be destroyed in seconds. Keep the trust of your parents, your brothers and sisters, and your friends.

    We love you. You have grown so much in the past year. You have grown intellectually, spiritually, and emotionally. Keep growing. Keep being kind to yourself and others. Again, because of your capacities, you can be a good example and friend to others. Happy Birthday!

Love,
Grandma Linda and Grandpa Winn

Birthday letters might be the best thing ever! The amount of love you feel from these letters is remarkable. There is something about a tangible message from someone you love that is different. I can genuinely see how much grandparents know and love about me. They are better than any gift, and I never take them for granted.

Sam, Grandson, 18

For each grandchild, these letters convey ongoing stories of growth, achievements, and trials. Moreover, they provide invaluable information about the unfolding of their lives from the time they could read through the beginning of their adult years. As our grandchildren marry, we also craft letters for their spouses.

The purposes of these letters are to give praise, present advice, provide counsel, forecast futures, express love, and wish grandchildren and others a happy birthday. We have attached several additional examples.

Visualize one of your grandchildren. Think about his or her upcoming birthday. Using one of the representative letters above, fill in the "Dear _____" with the grandchild's first name. Then determine how you would adapt the letter for his or her birthday. What would you keep? What would you change? How would you convey your love, thoughts, encouragement, advice, or praise? Use these sample birthday letters as springboards for your own grandchildren. Have some fun. Use your own language. Don't make them too serious unless that's what you are inspired to do. We promise your letters will be colossal hits. They need not be long or totally literate. They just need to represent your best efforts in conveying your love and giving a little advice. Most of all, make them your own sincere, unique creations.

Birthday Letter to a Granddaughter

Dear _____,

It is hard to believe that you have finished your first semester of college, have become an integral part of your work setting, and have come to feel comfortable around young men. Your growth since the beginning of your junior-high years has been stunning and breathtaking. Increasingly, you are discovering who you are, what you might become, and what vital role you will play in the unfolding of your life.

Because of your experiences with _____, you are now passing this legacy of love, understanding, and goodness to others. This is an impressive achievement.

We love your smile, savvy, grit, and love. Because you have significant capacities and confidence, be sure you combine these with the attributes of meekness, lowliness, and humility. This combination of divine attributes will serve you well in your desires to connect with, support, and love others.

Use the next few years to prepare yourself for living a contribution-centered life. We love you so much! We love the growth you have realized! And finally, a very HAPPY BIRTHDAY to one cute, competent, and caring granddaughter!

Love,
Grandma Linda and Grandpa Winn

Spouses of our grandchildren also receive these birthday letters. Again, this is another way of deepening relationships with all members of your family. Following is an example of a birthday letter for a grandchild's spouse.

We believe these letters play unique and influential roles in helping our grandchildren and their spouses sense our love and commitment. They also provide strong praise for solving challenging problems, dealing with failures, behaving courageously, and doing other demanding and worthwhile things.

Letter to the Spouse of a Grandchild

Dear _____,

What a thrill it is to have you in our family. We love how you interact with us, other family members, and also with _____. You are the perfect companion for _____. Your temperament meshes nicely with his. Your personalities complement one another and create a synergy that benefits you both.

We are so pleased that you know how to work hard and know how to save your hard-earned money. We are also very impressed with your capacity for planning ahead and setting worthwhile goals. These capacities and habits will serve you well throughout your lifetime.

Thank you also for the concern you show for others, particularly your own family. You contribute more than you know to their happiness and well-being.

As you move forward with your life, we know that you will be blessed with many sacred opportunities to help and support others. Because of your genuineness and sensitivity to others, you will be sought after for counsel and advice.

Finally, a very, very happy birthday to you! Please know that we love you through and through. Also, we stand ready to be helpful if you need us.

Lovingly,
Grandpa Winn and Grandma Linda

> My favorite family ritual is a meaningful letter on my
> birthday. It makes me feel good when my grandparents
> take time to express how much they love me.
>
> *Dane, Grandson, 15*

These letters give all our grandchildren and their spouses invaluable feedback about how we experience them and how we see them moving through each year of their lives. As you have noticed, they often provide advice or counsel. They always include encouragement. If you know your grandchildren and their spouses well, they are relatively easy and enjoyable to write.

Birthday Accolades and Tributes. In addition to the birthday dinner, cake, ice cream, and then blowing out of the candles, we often give all or several in attendance an opportunity to share something they really enjoy or like about a cousin, aunt, or uncle celebrating a birthday. These accolades and tributes are influential in their impact and capacity for affirming the positive qualities and behaviors of our grandchildren and their parents.

> One thing I love about being part of this family is being
> highlighted on my birthday. When everyone has some-
> thing nice to say to you, it really boosts your self-esteem,
> and you realize how many people love and care about you.
>
> *Sam, Grandson, 18*

Our grandchildren love the compliments and acknowledgments they receive from cousins, aunts, uncles, and us. The giving of these tributes helps grandchildren understand how they are seen and valued. Moreover, accolades support grandchildren's emerging perspectives regarding their strengths, talents, and positive attributes.

B-day tributes are where we go around and say something we love about those who are celebrating their birthdays. We all have different things to say because we all notice and love them for different things. These tributes make me happy to receive and to share.

Livie, Granddaughter, 14

Some tributes are funny, others are serious, and some are full of deep meaning. They help all our grandchildren see and feel how their cousins, aunts, uncles, and grandparents perceive them and their accomplishments. Moreover, the feedback they receive from their same-age or just-older cousins is highly prized and profoundly influential. We know this input from their cousins affects them very deeply and can potentially shape them in very positive and powerful ways over time.

Other forms of accolades and tributes come primarily from us as grandparents. As we learn about various kinds of achievements, accomplishments, and other particularly noteworthy behaviors of our grandchildren or their parents, we make a call, send a note, or make a visit to compliment them on their growth, achievement, or service.

We believe these small and consistent kinds of feedback and explicit expressions of appreciation shared with our grandchildren can and do influence the positive feelings they have about themselves. Moreover, they help our grandchildren determine what we really value and what we believe to be worthwhile, purposeful behaviors.

If you carefully listen, if you are attentive and watchful, you will learn about the things your grandchildren are doing and achieving that are worthy of your attention, acknowledgment, and praise.

When I am a grandparent, I hope to be as generous as Grandpa Winn and Grandma Linda. They take time to plan something for every event or trip. I also hope to be involved as they have been. They come to my athletic events, and I love seeing them there. I think that grandparents have the opportunity to make a big impact on their grandkids, and to do that, they must be involved, which is precisely what they have done for me.

Ellie, Granddaughter, 17

Do the Obvious Things!

For those of you who live close to your grandchildren, we hope you are attending many of their games, recitals, competitions, performances, and exhibits. These events give you opportunities to congratulate, support, and sustain your grandchildren as they learn how to be teammates, encounter challenges and sometimes injuries, and see how they are developing resilience and other valuable character traits. If you do not have an opportunity to attend these kinds of events in person, think about treating your grandchildren as sport's stars. At a distance, you seriously track their activities and performances. You learn and capture anything noteworthy about their performances, achievements, and aspirations. You cherish videos, photos, and stats about their performance. Then you find compelling ways to communicate your great pleasure with their accomplishments and progress.

We have discovered that our phones and cameras are invaluable in capturing various aspects of our grandchildren's sporting and other arts-related events. We then edit these pictures as needed and share them during family get-togethers as prints, posters, or slideshows, highlighting each child's achievements and challenges. These posters and shows are big hits. They also give us additional opportunities to praise the practice and other preparations that made their performances possible.

> Grandparents have so many roles in our lives. For me, my grandparents are part of my support system in my many endeavors. Whether it is a recital, sports game, or musical performance, I always have a grandparent coming or wanting to come.
>
> *Jane, Granddaughter, 14*

Grandkids cannot receive too much attention and commendation for playing, performing, competing, and behaving well. We pay special notice and give praise for acts of kindness, sportsmanship, bravery, and inclusion.

> There are so many different ways to be a grandparent. Just generally being involved can mean the world, whether you had a good or bad game. If your grandparent is there to greet you, it makes it ten times better. Having someone interested in you and your endeavors makes you want to work harder for your goals. It truly makes success that much sweeter.
>
> *Sam, Grandson, 18*

One of my problems in attending sporting events is my penchant for wanting to be a cheerleader, not only for our grandchild but also for our grandchild's teammates. I say things like, "Avie, I want your autograph!" "Nice pass, Payton!" "Awesome shot, Jane!" You can make a difference not only for your grandchildren but also for other youth who

may not have grandparents who can come and actively participate in their games and competitions.

Your grandchildren and their peers need all the positive encouragement they can get for playing hard, giving their best, being good sports, and so on. Don't miss the opportunities available to you to shape and support the next generation of youth, parents, and grandparents.

We make it a point after each event to reach out to our grandchildren and their peers. Our feedback is not contingent on their winning or their missteps during the game. We focus on effort, teamwork, giving their best shot, and playing hard to the end—in other words, enduring.

Your attendance and active participation at your grandchildren's many and varied events demonstrates your love and interest in them. Nothing says, "I love you" more than being actively involved in their lives and passions.

One on One: The Ultimate Gift

Some of the very best ways to lay down connective tissue with your grandchildren are one-on-one events. Briefly, here are a few examples.

🔆 I recently traveled with a twelve-year-old grandson—and him only—to a distant location to participate in a family river trip. We motored together for almost five hours. It was a total blast for both of us. He had my undivided attention. We listened to CDs produced by our daughter Mary Ann that captured her kids' favorite music and performing groups during the year. We sang together. We moved. We clapped. We laughed. We joked. We even broached some serious topics like what it means to become a man, what puberty entails, and what love is. His responses, as we talked, were hilarious and often profoundly insightful. It is safe to say that neither my grandson nor I will ever forget this time. It was a remarkably meaningful trip for both of us in so many ways.

The things I most liked about going with my grandpa were how much fun we had singing, joking, talking, and eating—lots of fast foods. I will never forget our time together. It was awesome!

Davidson, Grandson, 12

By the way, his own family members were delighted to have him out of their vehicle. On their way to the river trip, they enjoyed unusual amounts of quiet and pleasant conversations.

Another example relates to a fishing expedition I took with another grandson. We got a late start, and when we arrived at the mouth of the canyon where we intended to do some fishing, we discovered it was closed due to fire-fighting efforts. We headed back to a nearby convenience store to weigh our options. Fortunately, a bystander sensed our dilemma and recommended another location that was just minutes away.

When we arrived at the recommended location, we readied our fishing gear and began fishing. Before casting our first lines, we established a few bets or contingencies. The first person to catch a fish would receive a negotiated monetary reward. Also, the person who caught the biggest fish would be appropriately rewarded. We did not catch many fish, but the conversations we had getting there and going home were great.

The very best and most memorable part of the trip was my grandson's penchant for seeing me make hilarious mistakes while I was casting. I got my line caught in a nearby tree. I had my lure wrap around an adjacent pipe three or four times and then automatically unwind. His response to my antics was always, "Nice job, grandpa!" It was pure sarcasm. This is now one of his favorite sayings when we are together.

Some things that make good grandparents are these. They spend time with you. My grandfather often plays ping-pong with us. Sometimes we build model cars, or we have fun tournaments. He is also interested in our teenage words, our slang. I am glad my grandparents are a big apart of my life.

Gabe, Grandson, 15

One-on-one experiences with our grandchildren take many forms. Sometimes they are brief stints at a burger joint, ice cream parlor, sporting event, or pizza place. Often they are just a ride in a car to a friend's home, dance or piano lesson, or soccer practice. Sometimes they involve playing ukuleles, whittling, model building, weeding, snow shoveling, building, planting, or other related activities. These one-on-one experiences are generally accompanied by informal conversations about school, friends, and life in general. Because these conversations are relaxed and casual, they flow more smoothly than other kinds of talking or sharing.

Wherever your grandchildren live, close, or far away, there are many ways to stay connected. You may use any number of social media apps and other more traditional forms of interacting and connecting to nurture and sustain your relationships with your grandchildren and their parents.

What Should I Do Now?

Envision each of your grandchildren near and/or far away. Given their needs and current endeavors, what things could you do to encourage, support, and connect with them?

_____

_____

_____

_____

_____

_____

_____

_____

What could you do to connect more fully with your own children and their spouses?

_____

_____

_____

_____

_____

_____

_____

_____

Identify and prioritize several doable goals you wish to actively and immediately pursue. Also, set some appropriate deadlines.

Goals   **Deadlines**

_____

_____

_____

_____

_____

_____

_____

_____

_____

_____

_____

_____

_____

_____

Chapter 4

Disconnects and Reconnects

💡 For several years, we worked with college students at a major university. We gave leadership to their Sunday observances. We also contributed to their social, humanitarian, and spiritual experiences while they were completing their undergraduate studies.

We often gathered these students for retreats and other leadership training, particularly at the beginning of each school year. These training events were held away from their apartments and residence halls. We often met in a cabin not far from our home and the university. Dressed casually, we enjoyed a meal together and then provided team-building and other leadership instruction.

Every year, we began the training with a hands-on experience directly related to forming and sustaining relationships. We wanted these young people to develop relationships with one another. We wanted them to get to know each other well. We wanted them to build supportive connections with each other.

The experience began with a roll of toilet paper pulled from a backpack by one of the adult leaders on the training team. The leader then posed the question, "How and why are we going to use this visual aid?"

As you can imagine, the discussion leader got a lot of humorous comments in response to this question. Just think about what you might have said when you were that age. The leader encouraged the amusing comments and ensuing laughter as he saw the students begin to relax with one another. With the initial question and related comments behind him, he used the roll of toilet paper to illustrate some vitally important concepts about building community and personal relationships—about becoming and being good friends to one another.

The discussion leader holding the roll of toilet paper began by introducing himself—who he was, where he was from, something he loved to do, something he was actively working on to improve himself, and what he was looking forward to during the coming year. He then held on to the loose end of the toilet paper roll and lobbed the roll to one of the assembled participants, being careful not to tear the toilet paper from the roll. He then encouraged the receiver to share a similar introduction and toss the roll of toilet paper to someone else while holding on to his or her section of the strand of paper. Then, in turn, the roll was lobbed to someone else in the group until each had introduced himself or herself, and we were all connected.

We hope you can imagine how we looked with these strands of crisscrossing toilet paper and what the assembled students had learned about each other. With the last person's introduction and related comments behind us, we took a moment to link the experience to what we hoped would happen during the coming year.

First and foremost, we asked the assembled participants to think about the roll of toilet paper and the crisscrossing strands and what they represented. We asked them what other names were associated with this kind of paper. Eventually, they mentioned the word *tissue*. Yes, toilet tissue! Then we made the link with connective tissue. Once everyone was introduced and tied together with our connective tissue, we talked about what it meant to be linked and connected to others in helpful and sustaining ways.

Our goal that year was to lay down more connective tissue, to develop bonds, relationships, and friendships that would potentially last and influence them and us for years to come.

As the roll of tissue was tossed from one person to another, sometimes the tissue broke despite our careful efforts. This breaking was instructive for all of us. It represented the delicate nature of initiating and forming relationships and strong friendships. These breaks also highlighted the need for continually repairing broken, severed, or damaged connections. Friendships and relationships are often tested and diminished because of mistakes or errors in judgment. We wanted them to realize that repairs and restorations could and should take place.

Connecting with your children and their spouses is all about laying down connective tissue, forming bonds that initially may be fragile but, over time, become more robust if we are vigilant, constant, and inspired in our actions. Like the actual connective tissues in our bodies, they support and protect us from sources that may be detrimental to our emotional, social, and spiritual health.

Real Challenges

Up to this point, we have spoken very favorably and optimistically about forming positive relationships with your married children and their companions. We have talked much less about challenging or nonexistent relationships with married children and their spouses. We were concerned that some of our commentaries did not accurately reflect what some grandparents experience in trying to connect with their married children and their companions.

Disconnects

As we all know, relationships with children and their companions can often be thorny and challenging. Some of us struggle to make meaningful connections with our children and their spouses. Usually, disconnects with children's spouses begin during courtship periods or within the first few months and years of marriage. Reasons for this may be related to clashes of family cultures, generation-specific conflicts, or unrealistic/unmet expectations of all or some involved parties. Challenges also often come from ongoing or periodic fallings-out where individuals are offended, hurt, or otherwise disappointed.

You could probably make a list of things you think may be contributing to your poor relationship with a given spouse or one of your children. Or you may be entirely in the dark, wondering why that person wants to avoid you and chooses not to be connected with you in healthy and happy ways.

Candidly, developing positive and enduring relationships with some married children and their companions is challenging, if not impossible. Because of your children and their companions' choices, you may be prevented from having any meaningful contact with them or your grand-children. You may also have done some things that contribute to their ongoing discontent. Boundaries and walls may have been established that you cannot penetrate even with your best efforts. Despite your deepest desires to connect with them and their children, you are forced to remain on the sidelines.

You will need to determine what efforts you should devote to repairing, restructuring, or rebuilding relationships with your children and their spouses. In some cases, you will need to look for other means of connecting with your grandchildren—gestures, and actions that, over time, may give rise to fruitful and positive associations. These might include sending regular cards, emails, texts, small gifts, attendance at school, or sporting events—anything you believe will be well received and potentially helpful. Devoted and loving actions may be the ultimate keys to your eventual success in connecting or reconnecting with loved ones.

Reconnects

If you are wholly or partially responsible for the demise of your relationship with your married children or their spouses, we encourage you to apologize. Attempt to make things right. Seek answers to problems where each party benefits from the solutions selected. Pursue win-win solutions. If you have damaged the trust you once had, take steps to regain it. As you know, trust can be destroyed in seconds. Recovering it takes time—lots of time and dedicated effort.

💡 Our approach to addressing injury or offense is finding an appropriate time when we can meet in a private and quiet setting with those we may have hurt or offended. After we have exchanged the usual pleasantries, we try to move through four specific steps, usually in the following order. First, we verbally share our intent. This sharing may include expressions such as these: "We want to make things right." "We want to apologize." "We want to start over." "We want to say that we are genuinely sorry for what we have done and for any offense we have caused." "We want to ask for forgiveness." "We want to understand why there is a breach between us."

It is vitally important that you are clear on what your intentions are. Your children and their companions need to sense your sincerity in wanting to improve your relationships and connections with them.

💡 Second, we share our deepest motivations for improving or remaking our relationship. The following are some things we have said when trying to make things right with our children, especially when they were teenagers or young adults: "We don't always see things as you do." "We know we sometimes disappoint you, but that was not our intention." "Our motivation for having this talk is love." "We love you so much and want the very best for you." "We hope you sense our deep concern for you." "We believe we would be irresponsible as your parents if we didn't try to make things right with you." Statements like these let your children and their spouses know what motivates you to reconnect with them.

In expressing your motivations, make sure they are sincere and completely authentic. As we have suggested earlier, grandchildren and their parents are incredibly skilled in detecting hypocrisy and deceit.

🔆 Third, we explicitly describe how we hope they will respond. We encourage them to react positively, to assume positive intent in our interchange. Our conversation might sound like this: "Your first response to our expressions might be defensiveness or even anger, but we hope you will not react in this way. We hope you will weigh our sincere intentions and give us a chance to repair what we may have damaged, responding positively to our desires to make things right. Will you consider doing that?"

🔆 Fourth, once we have carefully moved through these steps, we listen carefully to their responses. Then we delicately respond by attempting to reflect what we have heard in response to our opening comments. You might say something like this: "Let me see if I understand what you are saying. You were deeply offended by our lack of sensitivity to your _____. You expected us to take more seriously your request for _____."

Once we are sure we understand what was expressed emotionally and what was verbally conveyed to us, we begin to address the problems. We attempt to see what specific things we can potentially do to improve our relationship.

Sometimes we use a "stop, start, and continue process." What should we both stop doing? What should we start doing? What should we continue doing that would help rekindle or rebuild our relationship with you and your children?

It is important to identify solutions that you both find satisfactory—again, you should look for win-win solutions. Depending on our need for closure, we often capture in writing what we have agreed to do. Then in subsequent chats or discussions, we can see if we have honored our commitments and if they have honored theirs.

We know that changing and improving relationships takes time and effort. Sometimes we must adjust our expectations as we move through the rebuilding process. We hope the process and related steps we have identified will help you make things right with your children and their companions.

Making the Best of What You Are Given

In some instances, your connections with those who have been distant or disaffected may be very sporadic and random because they live some distance from your home. However, as opportunities for visits come and go, do all you can to make them as meaningful as possible—the best they can be. Think about ways to make their time with you pleasant and positive, especially for your grandchildren. If they have positive experiences with you, they will want to be with you more often. They will encourage their parents to bring them more frequently to your home and related family activities. Your purposeful acts of kindness, compassion, and love sprinkled with lots of fun, and patience will convey your genuine concern for them and their well-being.

What Is Your Focus?

Sometimes your efforts will be focused primarily on your children and their spouses, not directly on your grandchildren. This will be especially true if your children and their companions struggle fundamentally with being "good" parents. They may need a lot of support in raising their children because of their choices as teenagers or young adults. If this is the case, you will need to determine what you can and will do to help them with their parenting challenges, and whether or not this help will be well received.

In supporting your children and their spouses, you might consider regularly providing some respite care for them. This might include assisting your grandchildren with school-related events, providing tutoring or other targeted assistance, helping with transportation to and from essential appointments, or providing additional support that responsibly contributes to their well-being and growth.

We currently help our children and their spouses by volunteering in our grandchildren's school classes, helping our older grandchildren learn how to drive, meeting with grandsons after school to build models, assisting with transportation to and from events, doing some cooking, helping with cleaning, and, if we are feeling fearless, helping with science fair projects.

As you might imagine, the level and kind of support you provide your children and their companions will depend on the type of relationship you have established and the kinds of needs they have as parents and couples. In some instances, your involvement will be monumental and almost full time. In other cases, your contributions will be modest and not that burdensome. You will need to determine what levels of involvement are required and what you realistically can do to help, support, and nurture them and your grandchildren.

Timing Is Often Everything!

In making connections with your children and their spouses, we stress the importance of doing it when it is convenient for them and their families. When we were newlyweds, we often received calls from Linda's mother quite early on Saturday mornings—the one day on which we had the luxury of sleeping in. Initially, we tried to sound as if we had been awake for hours. However, we finally let her know that calls later in the day would be much more appreciated and better received. As you regularly attempt to communicate and make connections, make sure it occurs at times that work for them.

Informal Dinners

One of our favorite means for connecting with our children and their spouses is a casual dinner at our home or at a convenient, favorite restaurant. We call these adult-date nights. We use these occasions primarily to listen and learn what is going on in their lives.

Usually, we let the dinner discussions naturally flow or emerge. We attempt to go where our conversations take us. If we feel confident and comfortable, we might ask about each of their children. We might ask about their work. We try to get a sense of how they are doing, what they need, and how we might be genuinely helpful.

When children and spouses live in a distant place, you may consider, as we indicated earlier in the previous chapter, sending them a gift card for a couple or family dine-out night or a special treat. Remember, connecting is about the tiny repetitive and meaningful gestures you offer that build and sustain relationships.

Use Social Media

There are additional ways in which you can connect with your children and their spouses. We mentioned earlier that we currently use GroupMe, a cell phone application, or Zoom, which allows us to communicate with all our married children and their families instantaneously. These are highly practical and easy-to-use applications. Moreover, the instructions for using the apps are simple and straightforward. With GroupMe, you choose a group name and an avatar (a representative symbol, graphic, figure, or photo) for your family group. Then you just add their names and cell phone numbers. Potential recipients receive an invitation, respond to it, and you are off and running. We have several groups—one for our children and their spouses, one for our college-age children, and one for the remainder of our grandchildren.

We use GroupMe for all kinds of events and announcements. We regularly send information that is of interest to all our married couples. It might be a reminder of an upcoming WELE lunch, an invitation to a family dinner with an attached food assignment, an announcement regarding the birth of a new cousin, an engagement announcement, or a report of some feat achieved by one of the grandchildren. We attempt to send these messages/texts at times that do not interfere with sleep—no late-night or early-morning texts unless there is an emergency that needs immediate attention. Our married children and their spouses thoroughly benefit from this application and use it a lot in communicating with each other.

Share Family Artifacts and Treasures

Another practice we have found to be very positive is surprising our children and their spouses with unique gifts, books, photos, or artifacts from our family. These have included long-lost but rediscovered photos, old report cards or school-produced crayon drawings or watercolors, math worksheets, papers from their elementary years, and early gifts given to us by our children's spouses.

One gift we recently returned was a prime piece of framed artwork given to us by our daughter-in-law. At the time, it represented her very best artwork. However, in the interim, she has made enormous strides in her painting capacities, garnering many awards for outstanding oil paintings. When we presented her with her precious gift to us, she was entertained, grateful, and glad that we had returned one of her more "humble" pieces of art.

Sometimes we provide mementos from years gone by—objects that represent critical or essential moments in time. One was a note written by our son while I was in graduate school. At that time, he was in the first grade. It was a simple note, written in his halting handwriting. He asked me if I was going to finish my dissertation that day. We had the note framed for hanging in his office. It represented a challenging time for us as a family. It showed the concern of a very young boy for his father, who was desperately trying to finish his dissertation.

You undoubtedly have photos, papers, or other artifacts that could be shared in meaningful ways with your children and their companions. As you attempt to simplify and tidy up your home, you will find precious objects that, when packaged and delivered correctly, would mean a lot to your children and their spouses as well as their children, your grandchildren. By sharing these unique artifacts, you provide a means for connecting your children to the past and giving them a sense of their present circumstances. Through these small remembrances, grandchildren come to understand what it means to struggle at times, what it means to be tenacious, and what it means to be an ever-growing human being.

💡 Some months ago, Linda selected and sorted many of her earrings, necklaces, rings, and other jewelry. Her intent in sorting these items was to provide her granddaughters with a very memorable experience. She wanted each girl and mother in the family to have several jewelry pieces that would remind them of that day and their connection with her. After a family dinner, she invited all the granddaughters and their mothers to a bedroom where she had artfully displayed the jewelry on a large, queen-sized bed. Each eager participant drew numbers from a vintage hat. With glee, each granddaughter and their mothers made their selections. Now, each had several pieces of jewelry that once belonged to Linda. As the pieces were selected, there was

often a related story tied to the earrings, bracelets, necklaces, or rings.

> When my grandma gave us jewelry, I got a whole set of star jewelry. This set included a bracelet, earrings, and a necklace. They have been very memorable to me and a great reminder of that day. I love having something that was my grandma's.
>
> *Rosemary, Granddaughter 12*

Connecting through Grandchildren: How Do I Do It?

The answer to this question is self-evident! Many, if not most, grandparents who live relatively close to their grandchildren attend their sporting, school, and other grandkid-related events. If your children and their families live great distances from your home, be creative. Ask for photos and videos that help you learn about what is happening to your grandchildren and their parents. Ask questions! Request recital programs, newspaper clippings, and other citations. Use Skype or other real-time apps. Remember, when you connect with your grandchildren, you are simultaneously connecting with their parents. This connecting and supporting comes in many forms. It includes attending all kinds of athletic games (such as soccer, lacrosse, baseball, and basketball), school plays, recitals, and other celebratory events. Attendance at these events also provides natural means for communicating with daughters- and sons-in-law. As you engage in these low-demand, easy-going conversations, you incrementally lay down the connective tissues that bind you to them and them to you.

We often take our cameras to these events for shots with teammates, friends, or other family members. We then send our best photos to their parents and grandchildren for their enjoyment. These small actions are part and parcel of laying down the connective tissue that links us together as families. Taking videos works in much the same way. They show your concern and desire to highlight the positive achievements and activities of your grandchildren.

Because these events frequently end just before dinnertime, we sometimes invite family members to join us for burgers, fries, and milkshakes. Regularly, other families also participate with us—the more, the merrier! Again, simple food activities are excellent means for fueling easy-going conversations and discovering what is happening in the lives of your grandchildren and their parents. These activities also allow you to meet their teammates, their peers, and parents.

Make Holidays Tension-Free and Joyful!

Many families experience much grief and tension related to holidays as they try to determine where they should spend their time on Christmas Eve, Christmas morning, Thanksgiving, and so on. We alternate years for major holiday celebrations and dinners. And even if we did not have this schedule in place, we would not make coming to our home an issue. Again, our focus is on cooperating and working together with our children and their companions to make these occasions happy and joyous.

Our relationships with our children's in-laws are pleasant and positive. At Christmas, we exchange small gifts and greetings. At special events such as graduations, recitals, performances, and other significant happenings, we join in celebrating our grandchildren's accomplishments and milestones. We attempt to work together. The operative word for us is *collaboration*, not competition. Grandkids and their parents profit from all grandparents working together in the best interest of each family. Try to make holidays and other important celebrations tension-free—times for really enjoying one another, developing sweet memories and affirming life-enhancing family traditions.

As we indicated at the outset of this chapter, there are many ways to lay down connective tissue with your children and their companions. At the heart of your connecting with them is discovering what they like, what they need, and what they want. We are confident you will be guided in your sincere efforts to develop enduring relationships with those you love so much, making a positive difference in their lives.

What actions should I take now?

Think about each of your children and their companions. Write down each of their names. What kind of relationship do you have with each of them? Carefully capture all impressions you have about their needs or concerns. Jot down your feelings and ideas as they come to you. Then give yourself some time to see how accurate and robust your impressions are.

Names

_____

_____

_____

_____

_____

_____

_____

_____

_____

_____

Once you have some certainty about what is needed to reconnect or connect more deeply, identify what you will do and the time frame for putting your ideas into practice. Remember, start simple. Select just one child or spouse. Make sure you are not trying to do too much too fast.

_____

_____

_____

_____

_____

_____

_____

_____

_____

_____

_____

Chapter 5
Family Traditions

Traditions are special events that help family members feel connected to each other. They provide grandchildren and their parents with reoccurring experiences that are highly anticipated and valued, giving rise to priceless memories that bind family members together. They also offer ways of celebrating important cultural and faith-based events.

Family traditions come in all shapes and sizes. These celebrations and gatherings are often tied with holidays and other engaging and meaningful events. Grandchildren look forward to these events because the traditions meet many of their needs. These needs include, but are not limited to, connecting with cousins and others, having fun together, demonstrating emerging talents, honoring special holidays, and developing vital social skills. These are also events that children count on, look forward to, and remember with great fondness.

This chapter will give you some concrete ideas about potential family traditions you could establish. Use our family traditions as springboards to determine what your grandchildren and their parents might enjoy. It may well be that you already have traditions that you can make a little more youth-centered, engaging, and entertaining while meeting family members' needs.

The Whats and Whys of Family Traditions

Grandchildren enjoy family traditions because they are pleasurable, genuinely meaningful, and packed with rich learning experiences. Great family traditions meet your grandchildren's needs because they provide a means for connecting with cousins, aunts, and uncles. Grandchildren learn about what is going on in the lives of older, same-age, and younger cousins. They also discover and develop essential social skills. These skills include knowing how to have meaningful conversations, how to listen well, how to ask questions, how to compliment others, how to solve problems, and how to share significant events in their lives.

Moreover, grandchildren know what to expect and what will happen during family celebrations and activities. They know how they will participate and what will be expected. As a result, they feel safe and comfortable with what takes place during these celebrations or events. Additionally, they may have opportunities to share emerging musical or other skills. Well-planned, purposeful family traditions contribute a great deal to the happiness of all family members if they are fun, activity-based, and meaningful.

The Purposes of Traditions

The most valuable traditions deepen relationships with cousins, aunts, uncles, and grandparents. They give grandchildren a sense of who they are and what they may become. They provide recognition for personal and family achievements, build family unity, nurture commitments for being good neighbors and citizens, and teach principles such as civility, integrity, and compassion. Finally, they provide grandchildren with potential role models for living out their lives with confidence and compassion. These role models might be older cousins, uncles, aunts, or newly married cousins.

Musts: Fun and Engagement

Family traditions should be entertaining and fun. This is the first threshold you must cross in planning and staging family-centered traditions. If your traditions are not intrinsically fun or enjoyable for your grandchildren, they will make other choices about where they spend their time and energy. Moreover, you will lose opportunities to bless and influence their lives for good. Invite your grandchildren to help with the planning and staging of traditions and related events. You will be surprised by the novel and engaging activities they can suggest and help stage.

Fun is exemplified in experiences that are upbeat, sometimes novel, and often include appealing foods. Our grandchildren love games of all kinds, friendly competitions, dancing, singing, playing and making music, crafting, and playing sports. Fun is almost always characterized by doing something that involves and engages grandchildren.

Family traditions must be action-oriented. They must be about doing, playing, and experiencing—not just talk, but authentic, hands-on, movement-centered experiences. These might include car races, scavenger hunts, pumpkin carving, swimming, hiking, building, weeding, painting, hammering, cooking, playing musical instruments, skiing, and like activities. They are memorable because they are appealing and full of antics, conversations, kidding, joking, movement, play, humor, mishaps, triumphs, and disasters.

The experiences of family traditions usually become the essence of stories told long after the events have occurred.

Making Traditions Easy and Manageable

Family traditions should be relatively easy to plan and carry out. Yes, some traditions may require extensive planning, but most should be stress-free. We often have our children and their spouses shoulder some of the burdens of more demanding events and traditions, helping us with food items and preparation, providing equipment, directing the cleanup after dinners, or leading games. We also deploy our older, high school, and college-age grandchildren in making the events doable and smooth running.

We'd like to share some of our favorite traditions to spark your creativity. Consider your own grandchildren and how they might enjoy these suggested activities. As you think about each one, consider the extent to which each represents purposeful grandparenting. Is it designed to help your grandchildren grow, stretch, learn, and become capable and caring adults?

> My favorite family tradition is to have Kids' Day once a week during the summer. It gives me quality time to bond and to do fun things with my cousins.
>
> *Dane, Grandson, 15*

Some of Our Favorite Family Traditions

Kids' Day. During the summer, we sponsor a Kids' Day once a week on the same day each week. It generally begins with grilled hot dogs and other foods our grandchildren enjoy; the picnic is followed with an activity. The whole thing lasts for about two hours. We share the responsibilities

for planning and hosting the events across various families.

For grandparents who work, consider hosting a Kids' Night or something similar. Do not be constrained by our suggestions. Use the Kids' Day idea as a catalyst for creating your own grandkid-centered events.

Kids' Days are incredibly fun. We sometimes go to a local, community swimming pool. We often have friendly competitions or quasi-Olympic events where Grandpa Winn gives grandchildren scores for diving and other similar activities. At other times, we play lawn games, do a simple craft, shoot hoops, or play Frisbee golf—whatever fits our interests and budgets. The grandchildren mostly entertain themselves during Kids' Days.

Our grandchildren, young and old, thoroughly enjoy this tradition. When older, college-age grandchildren join us, they simply enjoy the sun and being with their cousins. The success of Kids' Days is not dependent on having everyone come. Still, because they are so much fun, most families are regular and avid participants.

One of the great benefits of this tradition is the reprieve it provides our grandchildren's mothers. While the kids are swimming and enjoying one another's company, their mothers are talking and simply enjoying each other and the warmth of the sun. For them, it is a pleasant diversion from the usual demands of summer days.

My favorite Egan family tradition is the turkey bowl.
There are very few things I am willing and excited to
get up for. I have never been involved in anything as
inclusive and yet as competitive. Having fun is second
to winning.

Sam, Grandson, 18

The Egan Family Turkey Bowl. Another of our traditions is the
annual Egan Family Turkey Bowl. Held on Thanksgiving
morning, it began many years ago as a flag-football event.
So many participate now that we often have to create two
to three small football fields.

The turkey bowl begins with an early-morning gathering
at our home or a nearby neighbor's house. Before the actual
football games, we gather for hot chocolate, donuts, sweet
rolls, and fruit. After that, we head to the local schoolyard
with our boundary cones, flags, and footballs. We set up the
fields and then have everyone from eight to seventy-seven
line up according to their height, tallest to shortest. Then
we count off to form appropriate teams. We enjoy this fun
football tradition no matter what the weather dishes up.

Our goal is to involve all who wish to quarterback, receive passes, run, kick, block, or otherwise enjoy the game. We want every child, teen, and adult to have a family experience where winning is not necessarily the only goal. Our key objectives are participation and engagement. Moreover, we want all children, teenagers, and adults to have some fun, stretch themselves, show off their kicking or other skills, or call a few plays.

Each year, one of the great thrills is to watch Nathan, an adult member of our family with disabilities, run for a touchdown. He loves the attention and thoroughly enjoys being with his nieces, nephews, aunts, and uncles. The joy that all experience in seeing "Nate the Great" run for a touchdown or two is one of the best parts of this annual event.

The turkey bowl has a significant draw, often involving other families and neighbors. Each year, the event ends with a group picture—one somewhat serious and the other not so serious.

You may choose some other sport or activity that matches your grandchildren's preferences for a family tradition/activity. It may be an annual water fight, a soccer game, a board-game marathon, or anything related to your family and grandchildren's interests.

Pumpkin Carving. This tradition began long ago as we reared our own children; now, many of them and their families continue this tradition. It is engaging and completely fun. Each year, we cannot wait to see what they create.

The night of pumpkin carving is obviously accompanied by a lot of humorous conversations, bantering, and reminiscing—talking about previous pumpkin creations, related Halloween happenings, past costumes, and parties. We

suggest you use paint and paintbrushes instead of carving tools to decorate pumpkins for young children.

One tradition of our family is making sure that we get together the last Sunday of every month to celebrate birthdays and just have fun together. I love this tradition so much is because when I lived in Haiti before I was adopted, I didn't have the opportunity to see my family that often, and we weren't that close to each other. I love this tradition because it gives us all a chance to get to know everyone. Because of that, we can connect with each other so well. I love that we all have the opportunity to be each other's friends and not distant from one another.

Tanette, Granddaughter, 18

Monthly Birthday Parties and Dinners. On the last Sunday of each month, we gather to celebrate birthdays and holidays. Each family is assigned to bring a salad, dessert, vegetable, or appetizer, and we provide the main course. These parties and dinners generally begin around 5:00 p.m. and end between 8:00 p.m and 9:00 p.m. Our grandchildren and their parents love these dinners. They provide an excellent time for catching up, sharing recent family events, and enjoying great food together.

These parties and dinners contribute significantly to nurturing and sustaining essential relationships among and between cousins, aunts, uncles, newly married cousins and their spouses, and grandparents. Birthday letters are delivered (see chapter 3). We generally have a brief devotional centered on a character trait or valuable disposition. Our grandchildren love to gather in same-age groups just to talk and hang out with each other.

The most lasting and powerful features of these parties and dinners include stronger relationships, the savoring of treasured birthday letters, and tributes made to others by each cousin, aunt, uncle, and grandparent (see chapter 3).

Food-Centered Traditions

Many of our traditions center on food; the food has no special meaning other than what it signals about an event. Beverages and other food items clearly indicate that the meal is a family event. The smells, tastes, and food choices tell everyone that they are in their grandparents' home and that the fun is about to begin.

The foods that regularly accompany family traditions become representations of many things: fond moments with loved ones, significant celebrations, hard-earned achievements, and feelings of love and connection. Recipes for the following food items are found in the back of this book.

Egan Clam Dip. Almost every dinner we host begins with the Egan Clam Dip as an appetizer, a favorite with young and old alike. The dip, along with chips, is stationed in an area that allows several grandchildren and other hungry adults to "dig in."

We begin enjoying the dip as soon as the first family arrives. Informally, the dip serves as a potential motivator for each family to come on time—because those who arrive late often find that the dip is gone.

The dip area is a hub of lively conversation and is the launch area for the rest of the celebration. From the humble beginning of our extended family gatherings to the present, we have grown from two containers of cream cheese, one can of clams, and half a lemon to six packages of cream cheese, three cans of clams, and several lemons.

Egan Punch. Another family favorite is Egan Punch. It is served infrequently, making it highly prized as a beverage at family dinners. Our younger grandchildren really love this punch. We always have those who are not familiar with the punch guess what the ingredients are because its components are not easily recognized.

As our grandchildren mature and begin to bring their anticipated spouses to family dinners, they often ask if we are going to have Egan Punch.

Havarti Cheese. Another of our favorite traditions is Havarti cheese. As Great-Grandmother Marcia Egan used to say, "It's not a party without Havarti." Although we don't serve this as a part of every Egan family dinner, it's a food that reminds our grandchildren of their Great-Grandmother. They loved her and have fond memories of her larks, antics, and faith-centered conversations and devotionals.

Lake Powell Hash. Almost every year, we host an Egan Family Retreat. It may be tied with Thanksgiving, may involve a summer river trip, or may consist of several days in a large cabin. We reduce our preparation demands by inviting each family to contribute to various elements of the retreats. Some families bring games, and others bring special equipment.

One of the highlights of these retreats is "Lake Powell Hash," a traditional breakfast tied to boating and water-skiing trips to Lake Powell that our son-in-law Scott and his family enjoyed. The hash is now a favorite of the Egan family, and our grandchildren love it. Again, it represents a new breakfast tradition. It also represents Uncle Scott's love for his nieces and nephews.

"Chicken-Fish" Sandwiches. Another Egan food concoction is "chicken-fish" sandwiches." Many of our grandkids love this sandwich, usually made with fresh white bread, lettuce, pickles, and "chicken-fish"—canned chicken mixed with mayonnaise. When grandchildren bring friends to family events, it's fun to hear them describe chicken fish sandwiches and how much they love these sandwiches. The white chicken thoroughly mixed with the mayonnaise looks a lot like tuna fish—thus the designation or name: "chicken-fish." We have no idea exactly when we named this kind of sandwich. It just happened!

Grandpa Winn's Chocolate Chip Cookies. Our grandchildren also love Grandpa Winn's oatmeal chocolate chip or raisin cookies. They're very hard to turn down; it's almost impossible to eat just one. Again, these cookies represent their grandpa's love for his children, their spouses, and grandchildren. When grandchildren come to our home, their first question is often, "Did grandpa make any of his cookies today?"

Other Fun Traditions

Egan Easter Egg Hunt. Our annual Egan Easter Egg Hunt is a family-wide event that is usually accompanied by dinner. As our grandchildren become high school students, we have them assist us in preparing and hiding the eggs. Grandchildren are given a colorful bag in which to gather their twelve, same-colored eggs. Each of the eggs is filled with various items: candy, small toys, and other surprises. Each year, we add a few dozen eggs for neighbors or visitors who happened to be in the neighborhood at the time of the hunt.

After the dinner and egg hunt, we talk briefly about our religious beliefs centered on the Easter celebration. These brief discussions help our grandchildren consider their faith and aspirations related to living meaningful, purpose-driven lives. You, too, probably have faith-based holidays that you enjoy. Think about how you might make them even more memorable and meaningful.

Cheap but Really Good Dinners! Some years ago, we developed another tradition directly targeted at our grandchildren, who are in high school. Its purposes were multifaceted. We wanted to save our grandchildren and their friends lots of money. Moreover, we wanted to provide them opportunities to prepare a nice meal with all the fixings—a meal that they could rightfully be proud of. We also wanted to engage our preteen grandchildren in seeing this event up close and personal. We wanted them to learn about the nuances of dating and to have genuine fun with their school friends.

These dinners also allow us to discover what is happening in our grandchildren and their friends' lives.

Many high school students spend a lot of hard-earned money on dinners associated with various dances held throughout their school years. These dinners address the expense issue and provide many opportunities for us to connect with our grandchildren and their friends. This tradition has been embraced by most of our granddaughters and not surprisingly by several of our teenage neighbors.

With all the aforementioned considerations in mind, we decided to make our home into a steak house for our grandchildren and neighbors' kids. We refer to these feasts as "Cheap but Really Good Dinners." What makes them cheap is that the participating grandchildren and their friends prepare the steak dinners. Yes, steak dinners! Generally, we get things ready the night before the dinner. Our grandchildren and their friends purchase the steaks and other dinner items. They also prepare our home for the dinners. They iron tablecloths, vacuum, clean and organize things, set tables, polish silverware, prepare homemade rolls, and make a terrific dessert. Additionally, they make sure the barbeque grill works and generally learn a lot about cooking and serving a first-rate steak dinner.

Unique aspects of these dinners center on the waiters or waitresses. Typically, they are younger brothers or sisters of the dance participants. They also learn how to serve food, replenish drinks, clear plates, and serve desserts. They also get an exclusive preview of what it is like to date and all that it might entail in the future. They also love the tips they receive if they provide high-quality service.

In staging these dinners, we also learn a lot about what animates our grandchildren and their friends. We see how well they relate to each other. We discover what topics are important to them. We learn about their preferences and discover some of their concerns. Moreover, we come to understand how confident they are in learning new skills. They also get to know us. For some of their friends, this event becomes the launching pad for lasting relationships with older, wiser, mature adults—us. Unfortunately, some of our grandchildren's friends are disconnected from their grandparents; in those cases, we become their substitute grandparents for an evening or two—or even longer.

Some of our youthful dinner chefs call us months or years later for roll, punch, or other recipes. We are pleased these dinners have met a lot of needs for friendship, connections, and learning for our grandchildren, their friends, and us.

> One of my favorite traditions is the Christmas Car Races. Car racing is where we each get a mini car, and when it is your turn to go against someone in your bracket, you wind your car up and release it when Grandpa yells, "Go!" We do this until a winner is chosen, and we wait until next year when we can finally be on top again—maybe. We are all very competitive. When we lose, we all watch and try to guess who is going to win. The races are fun, and we all figure out who we are inside.
>
> *Livie, Granddaughter, 14*

Christmas Car Races. In conjunction with our family Christmas celebration, we have staged car races for many years. Our grandchildren and their parents really look forward to this part of the evening. In advance of the evening, we purchase "pull back" cars, trucks, or other kinds of vehicles for each grandchild and adult. These vehicles are wound up by pulling them back several times.

The races usually occur in a hallway in our house. The beginning and endpoints of the competition are marked with masking tape on the hallway floor. The length of the track is four to five feet. Almost any hard-surface space can be used for these races.

Each year, our son-in-law Scott (the Lake Powell Hash specialist) creates a double-elimination bracket for the car races. Incrementally, we move through each heat of the competition. Winners move on. Losers are eliminated. To date, very few adults have won the event. The young winners love beating their cousins, aunts, uncles, and grandparents.

The Christmas car races are rich with opportunities for grandchildren to learn about how individuals gracefully win and lose. These races also help our grandchildren learn about honoring rules, the importance of boundaries, the value of celebrating others' successes, and the importance of comforting those who have experienced disappointments and losses.

Devotionals. In conjunction with each family dinner or related celebration, we often have a very brief devotional. Generally, these devotionals center on essential topics related to character, faith, or some recent tragedy or neighborhood challenge. We often use a story, an object, or a video to introduce the topics and stimulate discussion. Some of our devotionals have been related to yearly family themes such as generosity, inclusion, courage, kindness, and other dispositions. Because the devotionals are short and engaging, they are mostly well-received.

Not too long ago, we gave each grandchild a small polished rock. The rocks came in all different colors. They were smooth to the touch and quite appealing because of their colors, luster, and size.

As a part of the devotional, we asked our younger grandchildren how they thought the rocks became so polished and shiny. We listened carefully to each of their responses. Then we showed them pictures of several rock tumblers and the grits / sands used to make them bright and polished. Then we asked them to connect the rocks and their shininess to their lives.

Quickly, older grandchildren made the connection that the problems and trials they experience in life will either rough them up or polish them—rounding their rough edges, making them very smooth and appealing people. As a reminder, we gave each grandchild and their parents a polished rock hoping that they would begin to see their tests and trials as polishing agents—experiences that would make them smooth and beautiful over time.

Consider Your Traditions!

Now that you know some of our favorite family traditions and their purposes, elements, and characteristics take a few moments to think about your family traditions. What are they? Are they engaging and meaningful? Are they fun? What would your grandchildren and their parents say about your family traditions? Would they give them a thumbs up, a thumbs down, or something in between?

What are your best family traditions?

_____

_____

_____

_____

_____

_____

_____

_____

_____

_____

What steps will you take to make your family traditions more enjoyable, meaningful, and engaging?

_____

_____

_____

_____

_____

_____

_____

_____

_____

_____

_____

What is one new family tradition you will launch within the coming months or year?

_____

_____

_____

_____

_____

_____

_____

_____

_____

_____

Chapter 6
Routines

Routines and Their Purposes

As you move through this chapter, think about your own extended family. What are your present routines and recurring practices? We invite you to use the ideas and concepts uncovered in this chapter as catalysts for designing, improving, or adding to your own family routines.

What's the difference between routines and traditions? Routines are everyday, repetitive things you do. Unlike traditions, routines are smaller in scale and not nearly as exciting. Family routines are repeated events and experiences that provide structure and meaning to family life. Routines include things like regular evening meals, cleanup crews, athletic events, and other recreational activities.

On a smaller scale, these family routines may include repetitive family practices such as blessings on meals, brief family devotionals, exploration of an important character trait, reflections about a family event or national challenge, kitchen-cleanup crews, and family prayers at the end of the day or at the end of an important celebration. We'll talk more about each of these later in the chapter.

The benefits of routines are many. They help grandchildren and others feel at home and connected to each other.

They give all family members events to look forward to. After all, they are useful, because they meet essential needs and informally teach very valuable behaviors and standards. They also help grandchildren feel safe and comfortable. They also give grandchildren regular opportunities to discuss pressing topics such as discrimination, racism, bullying, and other pressing contemporary issues.

Routines provide structure, so grandchildren know what to expect and what will take place. High-quality routines are rich with meaning. They convey love; reinforce vital, real-life principles; and give rise to family solidarity. They also prepare grandchildren for developing their own routines and practices when they become parents—and eventually grandparents.

One of the most potent effects of routines is teaching highly valuable social skills—greeting others, starting conversations, listening, understanding another person's point of view, sharing feelings, etc. We are continually amazed at the degree to which our younger grandchildren watch with great interest what their older cousins are saying and doing. They informally pick up all kinds of social behaviors and ideas about connecting and building relationships with others.

We watch with great interest as teenagers and even young grandchildren gravitate to the "adult" or the "young adult" table during family events to see what is being discussed. Often the topics addressed at these tables are more mature in nature and much more interesting than the typical child chatter at another table.

Our older grandchildren often talk about dances, dates, awkward moments, first kisses, and emerging relationships. These table discussions are highly instructional and helpful to teenagers and almost-teenagers in learning to form, nego-tiate, and deepen friendships with peers and others. They learn about the quirky things that happen on dates, at dances, at restaurants, and at other places where teenagers hang out.

We've been doing our routines for so long that they've become almost invisible to our grandchildren, our children, and their spouses. We'd like to share some of them, in no particular order of importance.

> Honestly, one of my favorite Egan family routines is talking with cousins, aunts, and uncles and getting updates on what is going on in their lives! We talk about all things, and it is so fun. I usually hear about some love stories, drama, and friend issues. Whether it is the old-est grandchild or the youngest, someone can generally help another out.
>
> *Jane, Granddaughter, 14*

Invaluable: Family Meals

If you are a grandparent raising your own grandchildren, you'll be especially interested in the benefits of this routine. This routine is essential for families of all shapes and sizes. It involves making evening meals regular, almost compul-sory family events. These are times when children, parents, and/or grandparents gather to eat, converse, and discuss the events of the day—and, when appropriate, discuss more pressing matters such as suicide, bullying, poverty, racism, abuse, and so on. These meals occur at a set time and place.

Family science research is compelling on the value and positive impact of regular family dinners. Families who con-sistently engage in this routine are more likely to experience less teen use of alcohol, cigarettes, and drugs. Furthermore, they evidence fewer serious behavior problems; decreased early sexual activity; better grades, higher self-esteem; less depression; and higher performance on achievement tests. These are outcomes most of us want for our grandchildren. This routine also nurtures and sustains positive family relationships. Families that consistently engage in this routine are more satisfied in their connections with one another— their relationships are better. As you might guess, we love this outcome!

While we enjoy our mealtimes together, we try to get a sense of what has happened during the day. Were there any problems? Were there any high points or things to celebrate? Did anyone experience any unique insights about themselves or others? Did anything happen at school, in the community, in the nation, or in the world that was distressing or noteworthy to them? The natural give-and-take of these dinnertime conversations gives grandchildren and others a means to make sense of the world around them and to understand themselves better. These conversations also give them a keen understanding of what makes others tick, what is excellent and praiseworthy, what is right and wrong, and who they are in an ever-changing world.

We often begin conversations with straightforward questions, such as, "What was something unusual that took place today?" "What was the high point of your day?" "What is the latest with Shane?" "Tell me something about your algebra class?" "How is your friend Sarah doing?" "What was the best part of your class presentation today?" "What, if anything, surprised you today?" The answers to these and other questions give you perspective about what your grandchildren are experiencing, what they value, what bothers them, and how they see their own and others' lives. Additionally, these relaxed conversations give your grandchildren time to reflect on what they are becoming, how they are growing, and what it means to be a caring person.

The attention you give to each grandchild during these informal conversations conveys the message that you are genuinely interested in what they are experiencing and encountering in their everyday lives. These conversations also help grandchildren (and others) develop the capacity to read or interpret others' behaviors and actions, thus helping them become more skilled in making decisions, assessing character, and reading the situations in which they might find themselves.

You will know you are on the right track when your grandchildren talk freely about their friends, themselves, and their experiences. Again, these discussions and other family-centered experiences help them become skilled in "reading" others, interpreting challenging situations, and responding with confidence when tested or badgered in some fashion by peers or others.

Prayers and Blessings on Meals

Because of our faith, we feel deeply about expressing our gratitude to God for His tender mercies and kindness. Our prayers are genuine attempts to express our appreciation for the blessings we have received and to thank God for the many angels in our lives—mostly earthly angels that reach out to us in our times of need, pain, and crisis. This reaching may come in the form of cookies, a snow-shoveled driveway, a phone call, a text, a card of encouragement, a warm meal, or a spontaneous hug.

Our family prayers generally take place in the morning just before everyone leaves for school or work and in the evening just before we go to bed. When we are on a family retreat, campout, or other similar events, we have one of the adults or one of the grandchildren offer the prayer. Through these prayers, we attempt to express appreciation, seek protection, invite inspiration, and acknowledge unique contributions made during the day by friends, teachers, cousins, aunts, uncles, grandchildren, and God.

Family prayers offered by teenage grandchildren and older married grandchildren serve many vital purposes. All of us need role models in our lives—individuals who help us determine what kind of men and women we want to become. This is particularly true of children and youth. They are looking for models, individuals, heroes, and heroines to emulate. Many of these models can and ought to be their older siblings and cousins. When they see and hear an older cousin pray with sincerity and real intent, it affects them profoundly. It touches them and shapes them for good.

Family prayers help grandchildren understand that we are in this world to help one another, to bless one another, to lighten burdens, to mourn with those who are grieving, and to be generous. In family prayers, grandchildren are taught not only to thank God, but also to voice gratitude for the contributions and kindnesses of others, to recognize acts of forgiveness, and to praise others for sacrifices willingly made. Our younger grandchildren have often brought us to tears or reverential laughter with their unique expressions of gratitude and petitions for help.

Mealtime prayers serve many of the same functions as family prayers. They give grandchildren, parents, aunts, uncles, and grandparents opportunities to thank God for the blessings of food and sustenance. Additionally, these prayers provide opportunities to express gratitude for other blessings received.

Fasting

Once a month, our families fast for two meals, usually breakfast and lunch. During that day, each member of the family goes without food and water until the evening meal. We share more about fasting in chapter 8.

The purposes of fasting are many. During the fast, we often pray for specific individuals and friends who struggle with health issues, experience emotional problems, or face other daunting challenges. Moreover, we may fast for inspiration if we are struggling with a question or problem.

We use the money saved from going without food to assist the poor and needy in our community. We contribute amounts of money equal or higher than the actual cost of the meals we would have eaten had we not fasted.

The blessings and benefits of fasting are many and varied. Grandchildren learn what it means to be very hungry; they begin to feel in a small measure what many children throughout our country and world experience every day. Additionally, they learn a measure of self-control. Lastly, they discover and potentially embrace a sound and elegant approach to helping the poor and oppressed in our neighborhoods and communities.

Hugs, Mood Elevation, and More

One of our most valued family routines is hugging. This hugging naturally occurs when we greet each other at gatherings: family dinners, athletic events, family visits, parties, celebrations, and other get-togethers. They also take place as we conclude activities or say goodbye to each other.

Grandma Linda's hugs were soft. They gave me an overwhelming feeling of love. As humans, we need physical
interactions to feel accepted and loved by someone.

Rebekah, Granddaughter, 18

The benefits of hugging are substantial and well supported by lots of research. They include but are not limited
to fighting stress-induced illnesses, boosting the immune
system, reducing stress, elevating mood, relieving pain,
easing depression, and strengthening relationships. As you
might guess, we really like the last benefit: strengthening
relationships.

For some people, hugging is not welcomed. ***Remember
that hugs must be wanted not imposed.*** Grandchildren will
let you know nonverbally and sometimes verbally if you
are intruding on their personal space. Letting someone
hug you is fundamentally a function of how much a given
grandchild or parent trusts you and your intentions. Also,
as already mentioned, grandchildren are savvy detectors of
insincerity. Authenticity and wholesome intent are everything in giving and receiving hugs.

Cleanup Crews

We feel very strongly about having our grandchildren
develop the attributes and behaviors associated with being
responsible and helpful. We want our grandchildren to learn
to be useful without being asked. We want them to offer
help in clearing tables, taking out the garbage, or being helpful. Ultimately, we want them to recognize how to be useful
without being asked. We want to nurture a natural capacity
and desire to be gracious and helpful wherever they might
be—at a friend's home, at a neighbor's house, in a classroom,

or elsewhere. We remember with fondness our granddaughters, Esther and Tanette, who spontaneously cleaned and organized their family pantry. Their mother was so happy when she discovered their freely given service.

When we have a family dinner or gather for several days of fun at a campsite or cabin retreat, we often form cleanup crews. These crews are captained or led by married grandchildren, college-age grandchildren, or older adolescent grandchildren.

We have a cleaning crew for each meal. Each team is responsible for creating a no-trace-of-kids kitchen and/or eating area. Individual grandchildren are assigned to these crews with specific responsibilities detailed on a well-placed poster conveniently placed on the kitchen refrigerator, tent, or camping table. Responsibilities or tasks include washing plates, pots, and pans, sweeping, taking out the garbage, wiping down tables and counter surfaces, and, generally, restoring the space or location to its pristine past.

On family vacations, Grandma Linda and Grandpa Winn would print out a list of cleanup crew groups. Because I was an older grandkid, I was often a team

leader and in charge of gathering some of my cousins to clean the kitchen. We would see how fast we could get each of the jobs done and helped each other pick up plates and put away food. It was actually pretty fun!

Elizabeth, Granddaughter, 23

We often say to the crew leaders, "True leadership is setting a loving and positive example for others on your team." We want our grandchildren to learn the value of serving, helping, and leading. We want all our grandchildren to become skilled in motivating and managing the simple behaviors related to living together and taking care of the usual tasks that precede and follow family meals and other activities. Also, we want them to learn to be responsible for caring for one another, increasingly choosing to be contributors, load bearers, and workers. We think these cleanup crews go some distance in helping our grandchildren eventually become responsible adults.

Early-Morning Experiences

This is one of the most challenging, rewarding, and scary things we do. Teaching grandchildren how to drive or helping them complete their necessary driving hours to qualify for a driving test is perilous and sometimes dangerous work. Fortunately, we try to limit our driving times to those times where the number of cars on the road is near zero—very early on weekend mornings.

I remember with fondness one of my first driving episodes with one of our granddaughters from Haiti. I determined that we would practice driving in a school, church, or shopping center parking lot only as fast as the car would idle. Even at that speed, I sometimes had my doubts about the wisdom of my attempts to be helpful as a driving instructor.

As you may or may not know, individuals who engage in shared ordeals generally become closer and tighter, especially if they are successful in realizing the desired outcomes. Such is undoubtedly the case with the driving experiences I have had with my grandchildren. First, they so much appreciate the time. Secondly, not all of our grandchildren's parents feel comfortable assuming these supportive roles as driving mentors. Third, there are risks and perils. One of our granddaughters who helped her younger sister accumulate driving time watched with disbelief as her sister abruptly hit a cement curb head-on and blew out two tires because of the speed with which the tires hit the curb.

Also, learning some specific driving skills is not without significant risks, even when practicing very early in the morning. One such challenge is parallel parking. Just the practice needed to parallel park between two cars is lengthy and demanding. And the risks of hitting the back, front, or sides of the other vehicles and your own vehicle are high and potentially costly.

> Learning to drive with my grandfather was mostly pleasant. I am sure I frightened him more than several times with a near, head-on collision, making abrupt turns then sliding some distance on loose gravel, and close encounters with other cars while learning how to parallel park. Yes, I made many mistakes learning to drive, but he was patient and was regularly entertained by my slip-ups.
>
> *Esther, Granddaughter, 22*

Having done this for many years, I can speak to the benefits. The grandchildren whom I have mentored were powerfully touched by my contribution of time and trust. The by-products of the experience were frequent laughter, elevated heart rates, and several near-death experiences—no, I am just kidding.

The best outcomes were deeper relationships and connections with each mentored grandchild. While we were driving, we often talked about other things—things that were important to them. These informal chats helped me understand what they were experiencing at school with their peers and teachers. I came to know them better. I understood more fully how I could be genuinely helpful to them. Then months later, after they had honed their driving skills and were licensed, we took drives together to celebrate their success in learning how to drive well and safely.

In summary, grandparent-supported routines are means for helping grandchildren understand themselves and others, learning new behaviors, developing highly necessary dispositions, building reverence for sacred principles and practices, and discovering their best selves.

You may have already established highly appealing and worthwhile routines for your grandchildren. If this is the case, kudos to you! If the importance of routines is new and attractive to you, begin to create and experiment with a few. See how your grandchildren and their parents respond. We think you will be pleased with your efforts and related results.

Consider Your Family Routines!

Now that you know some of our family routines—their purposes, elements, and characteristics. What are your present family routines? Are they engaging and meaningful? Are they fun? Use your discoveries to improve or create new routines for your extended family.

What are several things you have learned about family routines that caught your interest and attention?

_____

_____

_____

_____

_____

_____

_____

_____

_____

What steps will you take to improve or create your own family routines?

_____

_____

_____

_____

_____

_____

_____

_____

_____

_____

What new family routines will you launch and try?

_____

_____

_____

_____

_____

_____

_____

_____

_____

_____

_____

 Chapter 7

Yearly Family Themes

Purposes of Themes

Over the past ten years, we have consistently created family themes. For us, a family theme is a focus—a way of drawing attention to behaviors we see as essential to happy lives. Yearly themes are our way of showing our grandchildren what dispositions and traits we think are valuable and worthwhile.

> Our themes included things like "Reach Out to Others!" "Golden Rule" "Be Generous!" and "Choose Your Words Wisely!" The fact that my grandmother chose these themes says a lot about her and her desires for us. I wish she could still give us her words and advice, but I am satisfied with what she said and encouraged me to do.
>
> *Jane, Granddaughter, 13*

Each year, we introduce a new theme with one or several compelling stories that illustrate the behavior or attribute we hope our grandchildren will develop, embrace, and practice. Moreover, we make small, brightly painted, attractive wooden blocks with the themes printed on them.

Each family receives one of these blocks. We encourage each family to put the block in a prominent place in their home as a reminder and as a prompt for actively considering and developing the identified character traits and related behaviors.

Some of the themes we have pursued during the past few years include: "Kindness Begins with Me." "Manners Matter!" "Courage: I Can Do Hard Things!" "Reach Out to Others!" "Be Generous!" "We Are One." "Choose Your Words Wisely." "Do Unto Others as You Would Have Others Do to You."

Kindness Begins with Me

This theme was launched several years ago at a family gathering of all the grandchildren and their parents. We secured a cabin space where we could gather. There we spent several days and nights watching movies, playing games, enjoying great meals, and having fun.

Early on the first day of the gathering, we shared a very compelling story about kindness. Then we introduced the "kindness jar." We used the jar to gather "recognition cards" from anyone who experienced service from an aunt, uncle, grandparent, or cousin.

After each evening meal, we opened the jar and read the notes deposited by individuals who had experienced acts of kindness during the day. We talked about how it felt to

be treated kindly. We asked what motivated their generosity. We asked them to identify the best kinds of kindness for kids, parents, and grandparents.

Of course, the idea with the kindness jar was to increase kindness in each family. As you might guess, some families needed this theme and its application more than others.

In launching this theme, we wanted our grandchildren to know that kindness is a personal responsibility—it begins with each of us. As we increase our capacity to be kind, we grow in other vital attributes, such as compassion and mercy.

Be Generous

This family theme had its beginning in a book that we read about marriage some years ago: *The Good Marriage: How and Why Love Lasts.** The authors, Judith S. Wallerstein and Sandra Blakeslee, introduced us to the importance of generosity in happy and successful marriages.

As we discovered the vital importance of generosity in marriage and other relationships, we began to think about how we could nurture this disposition in our grandchildren and their parents. What stories could we tell to introduce the principle? What stories would our grandchildren tell us

*Judith S. Wallerstein and Sandra Blakeslee, *The Good Marriage: How and Why Love Lasts* (New York: Houghton Mifflin Company, 1995).

about their experiences with generosity? We also considered the degree to which this principle might bless our married children and their companions. We determined that this would be a good theme for our family.

We express generosity in many ways. To be generous is to be giving. When we sincerely give of ourselves to others, when we share things, when we provide care to the elderly, we are generous. We asked our grandchildren and their parents to think about how they could be more generous in their homes, at school, and with friends.

We often refer to generosity as *the sunshine principle*. Being generous is all about sharing simple gifts with others in our families, neighborhoods, and communities. These gifts need not be the kind you purchase. Generosity is about simply giving. It is about sharing yourself with others, sharing your light, and freely providing your time in others' service. It's difficult to assess the overall impact of this family theme on our grandchildren. Nevertheless, we know this theme intensified our relationship and deepened our connection with each other as a couple.

Manners Matter

This theme was one of the very first we put in place in our family. We had placemats made with a listing of as many of

the most highly regarded manners as we could generate. We used *Wordclouds,* a free program on the Internet, to design family placemats. We gave each individual in our family a placemat.

Following is a reasonably accurate list of the things we included:

- Open doors for others.
- Say, "Thank you."
- Compliment others.
- Greet visitors.
- Don't interrupt.
- Be a good sport.
- Chew with your mouth closed.
- Take turns.
- No double dipping.
- Put your napkin on your lap.

- Write and send thank-you notes.
- Be on time.
- Say thanks for a good time.
- Knock on closed doors before you enter.
- Make good impressions by being polite.
- Use good language.
- Be kind.
- Remember the golden rule.
- Say you are sorry.
- Let your hostess take the first bite.
- Say, "Please pass the salt."
- Say, "You are welcome!"
- Say, "Excuse me, please."
- Help clean up after a meal.
- Push your chair in when you leave the table.

Also, we made sure that each grandchild's name was printed on each placemat. Moreover, we included our names and the parents' names on each mat. We wanted each to know that kindness is an individual responsibility.

Interestingly, one of the best ways for your grandchildren to endear themselves easily and rapidly to other adults and friends is to be polite. Adults thoroughly enjoy children and youth who are respectful and have good manners. Polite behaviors readily catch the attention and spontaneously garner the praise of adults.

We have several grandsons who are remarkably polite when they are in our home or elsewhere with us. They are always quick to express appreciation for dinners, treats, and other fun experiences. When they exit a family event, we can always count on them to say thank you. We are confident that they are equally polite in the homes of their friends and cousins. We love the sincerity that always accompanies their expressions of appreciation. Also, we know their teachers, coaches, and friends' parents thoroughly enjoy their excellent manners.

Courage: I Can Do Hard Things

Developing the capacity to do hard things does not come easily or naturally to most children and youth. This is probably true for your grandchildren unless they are fully engaged in sports or other physically or emotionally demanding activities or pursuits. Providing experiences for your grandchildren that develop courage and resilience is very challenging and not quickly achieved. We have been mildly successful in our attempts to create experiences for grandchildren that promote courage, hard work, and resilience. The lessons are primarily work-related and tied to our home, yard, or garden space.

At best, we can say that we have helped our children and their spouses, as well as our grandchildren, become aware of the importance of doing hard things, and being of service. What follows is a brief description one of our granddaughters wrote about her experiences doing challenging and

demanding things—things well beyond her comfort zone. Before engaging in this service activity, she worked for and raised money sufficient to underwrite her expenses.

After I graduated high school, I knew I wanted to do something unique both to explore my independence and make a difference.

I chose to go to Africa because I couldn't imagine a bigger or more exciting adventure. I wanted to test myself as well as help the people in Uganda.

While in Africa, though, I did not have the supervision and leadership I anticipated. I taught math in a village high school, went white water rafting, jumped on a bungee over the Nile River, and helped plan and facilitate an HIV awareness soccer tournament attended by hundreds. Moreover, I frequently worked to stock and supply a medical clinic in a remote village and played with and nurtured orphaned children.

When I look back on my memories of Africa, I can't think of anything that has been more physically demanding and emotionally eye-opening. I think I became a realist in Africa. Many memories of Africa and my friends there are both painful and beautiful at the same time.

The bottom line is this: I went to Africa to both spread my wings and make a difference. I think the most significant difference occurred inside of me. I learned just how small I was in the world's scope and how overwhelming and seemingly unfixable so many problems are. I learned that if I can help or be kind to one person a day that makes a substantial difference.

Hannah, Married Granddaughter

Courage and resilience, by definition, are connected to mastering change, sticking to one's goals and aspirations, thriving under pressure, and bouncing back from challenges and setbacks. In a culture that is tied to simulated and mediated activities—mostly video gaming—it is challenging to create events that effectively compete with these games. Also, developing behaviors and dispositions associated with courage, hard work, and resilience is one of the most significant challenges we face as grandparents.

Most of our attempts at encouraging courage and resilience have been targeted at our preteen and teenage grandchildren. We focus these attempts on work activities at or around our home—yard work, weeding, planting, painting, shoveling, pruning, scrubbing, window washing, rock removal, bathroom cleaning, vacuuming, and so on. Most of these activities are outdoor tasks that require lots of effort and endurance.

Over time, we try to increase the demands and length of our work efforts together, gradually expanding the energy and time required to complete the tasks successfully. One of the most important things we strive to do is to model working hard and doing jobs well.

We work with our grandchildren. We don't merely provide challenging work opportunities. We actively join with our grandchildren in shoveling, weeding, painting, scrubbing, shining, vacuuming, cleaning, raking, lifting, pruning, hammering, building, planting, and harvesting. As we engage in these often demanding and sometimes fun activities, we are informally talking and chatting about how each task is connected to life. It is easy to make connections with fundamental aspects of life as they relate to simple things such as preparing the soil for seeds, planting various crops, watering them, caring for them, and finally harvesting them.

Our grandchildren come to understand that without planting, there can be no harvest. They also begin to understand the importance of pruning and its connections to producing healthy plants and fruits. Once they understand these concepts, they can start to think about the thinning and pruning that needs to take place in their own lives. They begin to consider who the pruners in their lives are and what essential functions they play.

Some years ago, we had a beautiful pumpkin on the brink of becoming one of our most prized Halloween decorations. Somehow, late in its growth cycle, the pumpkin became disconnected from its vine. As would be expected, it stopped growing. It was overcome with mold and disease, and it gradually sloughed away, becoming an oozy, sticky heap of slime. The grandchildren who observed our pumpkin's demise were quickly able to make connections with it and their own lives. Staying connected to the nurturing vines and sources of support in our lives is vital to our long-term happiness and success.

We often devote our efforts to service activities that require a lot of endurance, commitment, and hard work to address this family theme. We regularly involve our grandchildren and their parents in *The WALK* of the Juvenile Diabetes Research Foundation (JDFR). This daylong event requires a great deal of planning and organization. As a family, we join with other neighbors and community members to provide breakfast for two thousand-plus WALK participants. Several companies contribute the breakfast items. We set up the breakfast buffet, cook the pancakes, and make sure all *The WALK* participants enjoy a great breakfast.

As the day of service comes to close, we take down the event, pick up and remove the garbage, share the excess food with the local food pantries, and leave the space orderly and clean. This is a work-intensive experience. Our grandchildren learn a great deal from this kind of service, including what it means to start and finish a project well, what it means to be of service, and how it feels to give of oneself.

"Zillions" of service opportunities abound in our neighborhoods and communities for our grandchildren. These opportunities include visiting the elderly, working with a child or youth with disabilities, serving in food pantries, volunteering in "share houses," regularly taking out a neighbor's garbage, mowing lawns, shoveling snow, and tutoring refugees. In essence, the range of service opportunities is practically endless.

You want to engender this kind of attitude in your grandchildren: "How hard can this be?" "I've done things harder than this." Being able to respond in this fashion comes from experiences that stretch and test your grandchildren's endurance and work ethic. Be creative. Think about how you can expose your grandchildren to tasks, activities and services that promote grit and resilience.

Reach Out to Others

One of the more important things we do in life is to reach out to others. This reaching involves showing love and concern for others in small but essential ways.

When we introduce a family theme, we often share a personal story or experience that illustrates and gives meaning to the subject. Sometimes we find a compelling, real-life story that our grandchildren and their parents would find interesting and potentially motivating. Here is one such story:

A young mother on an overnight flight with a two-year-old daughter was stranded by bad weather in a Chicago airport without food or clean clothing for the child. She was . . . pregnant and threatened with miscarriage, so she was under doctor's instructions not to carry the child unless it was essential. Hour after hour, she stood in one line after another, trying to get a flight to Michigan. The terminal was noisy, full of tired, frustrated, grumpy passengers, and she heard critical references to her crying child and to her sliding her child along the floor with her foot as the line moved forward. No one offered to help with the soaked, hungry, exhausted child.

Then, the woman later reported, "someone came towards us and with a kindly smile said, 'Is there something I could do to help you?' With a grateful sigh, I accepted his offer. He lifted my sobbing little daughter from the cold floor and lovingly held her to him while he patted her gently on the back. He asked if she could chew a piece of gum. When she was settled down, he carried her with him and said something kindly to the others in the line ahead of me, about how I needed their help. They seemed to agree, and then he went up to the ticket counter [at the front of the line] and made arrangements with the clerk for me to be put on a flight leaving shortly. He walked with us to a bench, where we chatted a moment until he was assured that I would be fine. He went on his way."*

Our grandchildren immediately connected with this story. They wondered who this generous soul was. What motivated

---

*Edward L. Kimball and Andrew E. Kimball Jr., *Spencer W. Kimball: The Twelfth President of the Church of Jesus Christ of Latter-day Saints* (Salt Lake City: Deseret Book Company, 1977).

REACH OUT TO OTHERS

him to help? How did he feel after rendering his service? We then asked them to share experiences they had had with others that were similar. We asked them to share how they felt and what it meant to have others reach out to them. This storytelling set the stage for the launching of this family theme.

During the months that followed and as we met for birthday celebrations and other family events, we asked our grandchildren and their parents how they were doing in reaching out to others. We were often surprised and pleased about their outreach efforts to connect, support, and help others in classes, neighborhoods, and friendship groups.

We Are One

This theme had its genesis with Merritt Egan, my dad. He felt strongly about having his children and their spouses united in their interactions and treatment of each other. Like so many families, we did not always meet expectations in being united. We had our share of disagreements and altercations. As our own family grew in number, we wanted our children, their spouses, and their children to be united in helping each other, responding to challenges, and being there for each other.

Being one for us was centered on supporting one another in addressing all kinds of issues. These included illnesses,

financial problems, school challenges, friendship crises, and relationship issues.

We try to be united in our efforts to be with, strengthen, and help one another. We know all families encounter insults and attacks on their well-being. We want our children and their companions to realize that we are there for them. We also want our children and their companions to be there for each other when trials or challenges surface.

Another kind of oneness is expressed in our treatment of one another. Many of the other family themes we have already addressed are related to family unity. We want to be one in our expressions of kindness, courage, generosity, and love.

As we close out the description of this theme, we don't want to seem insensitive to the challenges confronting many families in seeking family unity. For many families, tragic histories of turmoil, contention, and abuse severely negate their opportunities for actively pursuing this particular family goal or theme. Again, you will be the best judge of what family themes will be the most appropriate for your family and grandchildren.

Choose Your Words Wisely

💡 This family theme might be viewed at first glance as the Egan anti-swearing campaign. That's not the case! Any use of profanity in our families is mostly inconsequential and infrequent. This theme was adopted because of the immense power of words in conveying love and concern, condemning others, affirming others, profoundly hurting others, and communicating understanding and possibilities to others.

We introduced this theme at a family gathering with several compelling stories, some of which came from personal experiences and others that came from fascinating accounts we had discovered. One of these stories came from my own experience. As a young child, I was burdened or blessed with large ears, depending on your perspective. Some years before I was born, Disney released the movie *Dumbo*, featuring an elephant with oversized ears that was also capable of flying. I don't recall the exact grade I was called Dumbo, but I do remember well the impact of the teasing about my ears. I was devastated and tried my best to ignore my peers' taunts and comments, but they continued for some time. Eventually, the taunting decreased, but the emotional scars were deep.

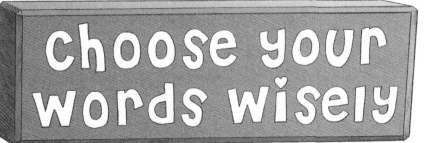

As I shared this personal story with our grandchildren, I learned they had never paid much attention to my ears and their relative size. They had no idea how burdened I had felt and how unattractive I found myself during my Dumbo years. Of course, even the name Dumbo posed some challenges for me. Fortunately, my ears are no longer a problem for me. Yes, I know they will continue to grow as I age, but I am now more comfortable with them and who I am.

Each of us experiences the impact of the words and expressions of others said to us or about us. These words may affirm or critically wound us or something in between. When we use our words wisely, we bless and support others.

As we continued our introduction for this theme, we wanted our grandchildren to think about things regularly said to them by classmates, friends, teachers, coaches, and parents. Had they experienced shaming or bullying? Did

they feel safe with their friends? We also wanted them to consider the things written to them in the form of texts and posts. We also challenged them to examine their actions—had they been guilty of any such behaviors themselves. Words and comments expressed by others can and do profoundly impact our views about others and ourselves.

We are not entirely sure about the impact this theme has had on our grandchildren and their parents. We do, however, hope that they are increasingly choosing their words wisely, blessing friends, cousins, aunts, uncles, teachers, and others with whom they interact—sharing words that build, affirm, and support others.

Be Picky

Because many of our grandchildren are now moving into their young-adult years and are actively dating and interacting with other young people, we created a family theme related to choosing friends and eventually companions.

Presently, we have five married grandchildren—three granddaughters and two grandsons. We believe all these grandchildren have made informed and exceedingly good choices in selecting their companions. We love their spouses and thoroughly enjoy the gifts they bring to our family. They

contribute so much that is worthy of emulation and application, especially for their younger cousins.

In setting the stage for this discussion, many months earlier, I had purchased multiple containers of plastic toothpicks—Linda's favorites. Our grandchildren were very familiar with these picks and often used them after a family meal. To stimulate their interest and motivation to engage in the opening discussion, I asked them to look at their toothpicks and guess what our topic for our brief evening devotional would be. As you can imagine, their responses to my question were funny as well as provocative. Quickly, I revealed that we would be talking about being picky—about being picky in selecting friends and eventually companions.

The stories we used to introduce this theme were by far the best we had ever used. What made the interest in these stories so remarkably high? The answer is simple. We invited each newly married couple to tell their cousins about their courting experiences and how they "picked" their spouses.

Each talked about what they were looking for in a spouse and why each factor was so important. Also, each related experiences that were pivotal in finalizing his or her choice. We then had our children and their spouses share their selection stories as well. The evening was rich with meaning and motivation because of the personal nature of the stories.

> Each of our family themes was a great reminder to be kind, to be better, and to love more. Family parties and trips were centered on a theme that carried throughout the whole year. The themes really brought the family together and helped put everyone on the same page— they were just excellent reminders to be good people.
>
> *Abby, Granddaughter, 20*

Summary Comments about Themes

We believe family themes serve several useful purposes. First, they communicate and affirm truths, principles, and ideals that are important to us as grandparents. It is our way of saying and pointing out what is important to us. It is our means of identifying dispositions and behaviors that we believe are foundational to happy and meaningful lives.

Over time, we have discovered this: to derive the best benefits from these themes, we must continually revisit and discuss them. In the absence of regular reviews, we were unlikely to see much change in our grandchildren and their parents' attitudes and behaviors.

Second, building interest in each theme is tied to the power of the stories selected to launch each topic. The very best stories are those that come from your own families and their experiences. These stories set the stage for engaging your grandchildren and motivating them to listen more actively than they would otherwise. Our married grandchildren's stories about their courting and spouse selection represent the kind of stories we recommend.

Third, the wooden blocks with the themes printed on them serve as reminders for applying the concepts. However, they are not that useful unless the parents actively use them to remind, encourage, and support the behaviors associated with each topic in their homes.

Lastly, family themes set the stage for continuing traditions and rituals that may be embraced by your grandchildren as they form their own families and eventually have their own children and grandchildren. Their practices as parents and as future grandparents have their beginnings with you. Preparing your grandchildren to be purposeful parents and grandparents is sacred work.

A Few Questions for Your Consideration

What struck you about this chapter and its focus on family themes? What thoughts and ideas came to you as you moved through this chapter? Have you thought about one or two themes that might be appropriate for your family?

_____

_____

_____

_____

_____

_____

_____

What do you really want to remember about the information in this chapter?

_____

_____

_____

_____

_____

_____

_____

What are the essential elements of effectively launching family themes?

_____

_____

_____

_____

_____

_____

_____

_____

_____

_____

_____

Chapter 8

Building Spirituality in Your Grandchildren

What Is Spirituality?

What is spirituality, especially in children and youth? And why would grandparents be interested in nurturing spirituality or contributing to the development of spirituality in their grandchildren?

Before we attempt to answer these questions, we want to share several statements about our intent. We are not trying to encourage any specific form of spirituality. Spirituality is a highly individual and personal matter. As indicated earlier, spirituality and inspiration manifest themselves in many ways and emanate from many sources.

We want to share with you what we have done—nothing more and nothing less. Again, it is not our intent to promote any specific approach to spirituality. We wish to share with you some of our practices in nurturing spirituality in our grandchildren. As you explore these practices, you will discover some elements of our faith and related beliefs—because this is who we are and what we value. We know you will be wise enough to determine what will work best for you and your family.

We have learned from our own experiences that we benefit significantly from divine help and guidance. We refer to this divine help as inspiration. From our perspective, we believe that inspiration is vital to our success in serving as caring and devoted grandparents. Regularly, we have been helped by divine inspiration in addressing individual and family problems, making important decisions, and selecting various approaches for assisting and supporting our grandchildren and their parents.

Now let's address the questions we posed at the beginning of this chapter. From our perspective, *spirituality* is a deep feeling of being right with God, friends, neighbors, and oneself. It is also the capacity to receive guidance for conducting one's life. It is the ability to access support in making decisions, discovering one's deepest purposes in life, and becoming contemplative, other-centered beings. Moreover, it is a disposition to be genuinely helpful to others. It is freely sharing one's talents and means for fighting injustice, helping others, and becoming our best selves.

Spirituality is a multifaceted concept. Its highest purposes are rooted in being moral and upright in our actions with others, especially with those different from ourselves. It centers on loving those around us. It is rooted in integrity. It is the capacity to feel and respond fully and accurately to divine intimations, influences, and promptings.

Spirituality is also a form of light that others experience when they encounter a genuinely good person. We believe this light is tangible and uplifting. It calms, inspires, and heals. It manifests itself in compassion, tolerance, kindness, forgiveness, patience, inclusion, and generosity.

Think about your views of spirituality and the sources of inspiration in your life. How would you define spirituality in your own life? What gives rise to inspiration and meaning in your life? As you answer these questions, ideas for nurturing spirituality in your grandchildren will come to you. With these ideas in mind, please join us as we review our approaches for encouraging spirituality in our grandchildren. See what resonates with you!

We want our grandchildren to be familiar with spirituality—its sources, benefits, and splendors. We want them to have access to the power of inspiration in making essential decisions, guiding their lives, and blessing others. We want them to have a clear sense of purpose. We want them to find meaning in the lives they pursue. We believe spirituality and inspiration are essential to a happy and fulfilling life.

Spirituality Begins with You

Because we believe spirituality is central to our happiness and our primary purposes in life, we are committed to helping our grandchildren build this essential attribute. Our attempts to nurture spirituality in our grandchildren occur in many ways. First and foremost, we strive to be worthy of emulation. We try to evidence spirituality in our lives that speaks to our grandchildren. To say it in another way, we try to exemplify spirituality in our interactions with them and others.

We attempt to be genuinely kind to one another and others. We try to honor God with the choices and the behaviors we manifest. We try to radiate light that calms, instructs, and inspires. We try to be authentically moral in our actions. Of course, we are not always successful. Still, we sincerely strive to have our efforts consistently represent our deepest beliefs and values.

Discovering and Encouraging the Divine within Each Grandchild

In building spirituality in our grandchildren, we first attempt to help them discover the divine within them. We believe that each of us is blessed with a natural, God-given light—a capacity to know what is worthwhile, right, and moral. It is a remarkable form of conscience. We try to sensitize our grandchildren to this divine gift—this light and this capacity to know and do what is right. This gift also helps them understand what is wrong, evil, and immoral.

Given this belief, we encourage our grandchildren to use this sacred gift in the service of others, their families, and themselves. Again, we believe all children—in fact, all individuals—are blessed with this light. However, we believe this light must be nourished, or it will fade or disappear. Our job is to help them discover it and be consistently responsive to it. As we mentioned earlier, this light is a divine source of conscience. It is a matchless, incomparable gift.

Developing Spirituality in Grandchildren

🔆 For years, I have attempted to grow this gift and other spiritual dispositions in our grandsons. As each grandson begins his senior year of high school, I ask him if he wants to devote a regular time each week before the school day starts to explore various spiritual topics. These topics include serving others, praying with real intent, pondering, meditation, reading sacred texts, and thoroughly studying concepts such as mercy, forgiveness, tolerance, restitution, restoration, redemption, compassion, justice, privilege, generosity, captivity, liberation, and justice.

Settings aside a regular time to study with my grandpa was very beneficial for my spiritual growth and other aspects of my life. I was able to see what he values and the morals he has and how he applies these in his life. Thanks to these early mornings, I discovered what I valued and bettered my personal moral compass.

Jacob, Grandson, 21

We generally met for about thirty minutes each week. We began and closed our studies and discussions with prayers and expressions of gratitude. The experiences I have had with my grandsons have been remarkably powerful and enlightening for me.

As we moved through the year with our studies and discussions, we came to understand the importance of fervent prayers. We deepened our connections with others. Life's moral imperatives became more apparent and clear to us. We discovered the essential value of acting on our spiritual impressions.

Often, I exited these mornings with a deep sense of gratitude that I was permitted to be with my grandsons, who eventually will become caring and responsible men, husbands, and fathers. This regular time was as much about becoming good men as it was about seeking and receiving inspiration and growing spiritually.

More recently, I have been meeting with one of my granddaughters, Rebekah. Together we have explored and discussed similar topics as I did with my grandsons. We followed the same format with prayers and candid, interest-driven discussions. Again, I came away from these weekly discussions with a profound sense of gratitude for having the opportunity to feel deeply connected with this grand-daughter and to shape her future as a vibrant, caring woman.

Seeking Divine Help and Expressing Gratitude

In our family, seeking divine help comes through pray-ing, pondering, and attempting to live in concert with our deeply held beliefs and values. As mentioned previously, prayers before meals, family prayers, and personal prayers are consistently part of our family routines. However, we try not to make the prayers themselves routine.

Most of our prayers center on expressing appreciation for blessings in our lives, asking for help with family challenges, petitioning God for help with dear friends and others in our community or elsewhere in the world who are suffering, and seeking assistance for the challenges of any given day. We also use our family prayers to express appreciation for acts of kindness and generosity shown by our grandchil-dren, their parents, and others. Prayers also accompany our fasting efforts for family members, neighbors, and others who are burdened or challenged with physical, emotional, health, financial, or other serious issues.

Serving Others

We believe service to others is essential to living well and developing spirituality. This service begins in the family, extends to neighbors, and spreads out to the community and beyond. Our service occurs on many levels. Our grand-children love assisting with various events that are centered on refugees and their families. Almost every grandchild is skilled in face painting, preparing and serving food, raising funds for worthwhile causes, and cleaning up after large-scale and not-so-large-scale events.

Each year, we provide dinners for young people from Chicago who are cancer survivors or who are successfully negotiating the challenges posed by cancer or other health conditions. Through agency sponsorships and additional funding, these youth enjoy an exciting week and participate in a variety of adventures depending on the season of the year. These may include skiing, camping, snowboarding, hiking, and river running.

Our children and their children, as well as other volunteers, regularly provide and serve evening meals during their weeklong stays. Recently, our grandchildren and their parents also participated in some after-dinner games, which they thoroughly enjoyed. These service experiences teach our grandchildren a great deal about others, their challenges, and their courageous responses to cancer and other related health conditions. Additionally, they learn how important it is to connect with others, discover their needs, provide thoughtful service, and be inclusive.

We believe you cannot help others without feeling a sense of satisfaction, fulfillment, and happiness yourself. One of the most significant sources of spirituality for our grandchildren is their service to others. You can play useful roles in helping your grandchildren serve others in a host of neighborhood and community enterprises.

As you know, your behavior and example powerfully teach what it means to be spiritual—to be service-oriented. Get your grandchildren engaged! Service can bless all of us in remarkably beneficial and powerful ways.

Inspirational Texts, Literature, and Media

🕯 We also attempt to help our grandchildren develop spirituality by exposing them to sacred texts, inspirational literature, and media. We try not to be heavy-handed in these development efforts. We try to find simple, stirring stories, and other materials that naturally provide a means for talking about justice, compassion, charity, forgiveness, healing, inclusion, and redemption. One of our favorite videos features a six-year-old boy, Jaden Hayes, who lost both parents early and quickly in his life. In a *YouTube* video clip,* Jaden speaks about his attempts to share happiness with others after the passing of his parents.

Jaden's story touched our grandchildren and their parents. It also provided an excellent opportunity for us to talk about death and the ways profound grief can be turned into joy. Videos like this one can move grandchildren to think about and act in ways that comfort, heal, and bless others. These kinds of stories, video clips, and other media also motivate actions that otherwise would not be considered or pursued.

The Power of Music

We believe music is one of the most potent means of feeling and expressing spirituality. We have a family song that we often sing in conjunction with sacred events. These events include saying goodbye to grandchildren who are going away to school, conveying courage to couples or grandchildren who are exiting for a time to give service in a faraway land or region, and expressing love and peace on special occasions, including funerals, weddings, or other celebrations.

Our family song is one of our sacred and most treasured traditions. You may want to consider selecting a piece of

---

*CBS Evening News, *On the Road with Steve Hartman*, https://www.youtube.com/watch?V=OCPc2RIMTll.

music that inspires you and your grandchildren. Then it can become a regular part of family events during which the music may be helpful and inspirational to those celebrating a significant event, moving to a new community, or preparing for a challenging adventure or service.

Seeking Spirituality through Fasting and Contributions

Earlier, we mentioned our family efforts to fast regularly. We believe fasting contributes to spirituality in significant ways. As you know, fasting is a common practice in many cultures and religions. Fasting achieves many worthwhile spiritual purposes. These include a heightened awareness of our dependence on food and water, a means for understanding others who have considerably less, and potentially profound access to spiritual impressions and guidance. Fasting is also a means for expressing gratitude, a process leading to greater self-control, a method for seeking help for others, and an avenue for cleansing and renewal. These are some of the benefits we have found from fasting.

Families who come together to fast realize significant blessings in many domains, as do those for whom they have fasted. Imagine what would happen if each family in the world who is blessed with abundance and prosperity regularly contributed the money saved by fasting for humanitarian causes such as hunger, homelessness, and education. The results could be staggering! Fasting is and can be an elegant way of helping others—even your grandchildren. Give it a try!

In summary, you can help your grandchildren develop spirituality. You can support them in becoming individuals who emanate a light that heals, calms, and brings peace to others. Understandably, your path and their route to spirituality are distinctively personal. You begin by mirroring or reflecting goodness and light in your own lives. You then help them discover and nurture their own inherent light. Over time, they become a source of peace and healing to others—their friends, parents, and others.

We conclude with one verse of one of our favorite family songs, "This Little Light of Mine," by Harry Dixon Loes:

> This little light of mine, I'm gonna let it shine,
> This little light of mine, I'm gonna let it shine,
> This little light of mine, I'm gonna let it shine—
> Let it shine, Let it shine, Let it shine.

We believe all of us are blessed with this little light. As grandparents, we want to nurture this inner light in our grandchildren. We want to support and encourage them to become individuals who are full of integrity, goodness, and light. And who emanate this light in their actions with others.

Capture Your Feelings and Thoughts

What struck you as you moved through this chapter?

_____

_____

_____

_____

_____

_____

_____

_____

_____

What inclinations do you have at this moment? What might you do in response to what you have felt?

_____

_____

_____

_____

_____

_____

_____

_____

_____

_____

What kinds of light would you like your grandchildren to radiate in living with and relating to others?

_____

_____

_____

_____

_____

_____

_____

_____

_____

_____

Chapter 9

What Do Grandchildren Want and Need?

The Wants and Needs of Grandchildren

By necessity, this chapter restates and amplifies content presented in earlier chapters. Let's first begin by talking about wants and later about needs. What do your grandchildren want? Often their wants are frivolous and not that meaningful in the whole scheme of things. Sometimes, their wants are very specific or driven by a particular craze or fashion preference.

For a moment, think about what your grandchildren would say if you asked them: "What do you most want from me?" Or, "What do you most want from us?" We have found that grandchildren, even older grandchildren, have a difficult time understanding and making sense of this question. However, we want to share what we think they want from you.

We feel strongly that your grandchildren want you—your attention, praise, feedback, and encouragement. Fundamentally, they want you to connect with them. They want to have meaningful and healthy relationships with you.

They Want Quality Connections

As you might imagine, your grandchildren want positive connections with you. They want relationships with you.

They want the "connective tissue" that we described in chapter 4. In the absence of well-established, positive relationships with you, they probably don't want much from you.

> I was lucky enough to live in my grandfather's home for a year while finishing my bachelor's degree and launching my career. Every morning when I would wake up and come down to the kitchen to make breakfast, Grandpa Winn would leave a little note of love and encouragement on a whiteboard. Some of the most memorable were, "I love your grit." "You are an example to me." "I love how motivated you are." "You are C squared!" [You are comprehensively cute]." These messages of love and encouragement were the perfect way to make me feel important and loved.
>
> *Eliza, Granddaughter, 21*

We believe most grandchildren desperately want to be connected with you. High-quality relationships develop as grandparents do these things:

- Listen carefully with the intent to understand.
- Discover and respond appropriately to their grandchildren's needs.
- Act with true authenticity.
- Actively engage and participate in the lives and pursuits of their grandchildren.
- Affirm the development of their grandchildren's skills, dispositions, and knowledge.
- Support their talent development.
- Give them a sense of confidence and control.
- Help them feel significant—help them feel loved.

Grandchildren also want these things from grandparents:

- Advice and counsel—they want your take on some, but not all, things.
- Enduring connections.
- Experiences that inspire, motivate, and engender trust, confidence, and competence.
- Input about boundaries and standards of living meaningful lives
- A sense of who they are and what their heritage is.

They Want to Be Heard and Understood

Listening well requires much effort and sensitivity. You need to be fully present when you are listening. Listening is intensive work: Your speech and actions demonstrate that you are focused on what grandchildren have to say and what they are feeling.

Sometimes listening to grandchildren is inconvenient. When grandchildren want to talk, it is a good practice to listen immediately and take them seriously. When they want to share their feelings and concerns, you must be willing and prepared to give them the time and attention they need.

When grandchildren have the sense you are there for them, you can learn incredible things about their triumphs, concerns, and aspirations. I am often struck by what I can learn when interacting informally with a grandson or granddaughter while we are weeding, cleaning, or planting.

💡 I recall with great clarity many conversations I had with one of my granddaughters. These often occurred while we were working together—cleaning our kitchen or weeding our flowerbeds. Without any prompting, the words just flowed.

I learned about her school experiences. I heard about emerging relationships. She mostly talked. I mostly listened. Occasionally, I attempted to see if what I was hearing was what she was saying. I asked something like, "Is this what is happening?" or "Do I have this right, is this what you were feeling at the time?" I followed these questions by sharing what I received and understood. I attempted to determine if what I heard was accurate.

If you provide the right environment, your grandchildren will share much of their lives with you. Sharing begins with establishing trust with each grandchild. You do this by being reliable, by keeping confidences, listening more than talking, and reflecting back what you believe you have heard. It is a good idea to remember what you have learned from your conversations and informal observations. Not that you need to take notes—you just carefully attempt to determine, feel, and capture what is going on in each of your grandchildren's lives. As you listen well, you begin to understand what they want and need. You become more capable of responding to their needs because you know what they are. You come to understand how you can help them grow and change. You understand how you can be genuinely supportive of them in realizing their aspirations and desires.

They Want Authenticity

We have devoted considerable space to this topic. Grandchildren want grandparents who are sincere and believable in their talk and actions. They'll immediately know if you are insincere. This is especially true for teenagers. They have a keen sense of fidelity and genuineness. They can identify a fake very rapidly.

If you have been less than authentic in the past, own this with your grandchildren. Let them know that you are trying to be more sincere and genuine. Then do all you can to have your good intentions match your behaviors, actions, and expressions. Strive for complete agreement between your good desires and related actions. One last piece of advice—stay away from sarcasm. Children, especially young children, are confused with statements that appear to be positive or affirming but are not.

They Want You to Be Engaged and Involved

Again, we have spoken at length about being an active part of your grandchildren's lives. You are engaged when you make every effort to be a part of their activities. If you are hundreds or thousands of miles away from your grandkids, you will have to be more creative. You may need to treat them like a sports star you followed as a kid. You know their box scores. You know if they hit a home run, made a three-pointer, danced in a school event, performed in a band or choir, or improved on their best personal time in a track event.

Grandchildren profit significantly from your presence at performances—recitals, spelling bees, award ceremonies, art exhibits, etc. As you discover these accomplishments, you make every effort to express your pleasure and excitement about their achievements. These expressions can come in the form of texts, phone calls, virtual video chats, and so on. Don't forget to be alert for remarkably impressive behaviors related to your grandchildren's generosity, sportsmanship, and compassion.

If you live near your grandchildren, you will want to make every effort to be present at their games, recitals, performances, and competitions. Your presence means a lot. The only thing better than a parent or a peer cheering you on is a grandparent's voice of encouragement and support.

💡 We recently attended a jazz concert that featured bands composed of young teenagers, two of whom were our grandsons. They were all decked out. One wore a black fedora, black shirt, white tie, and pinstriped coat. He played in the trombone section with other young musicians. The other grandson sported a black jacket with a bright red shirt. He played bass guitar. They both looked great. Their bands wowed the audience and us with their virtuosity and talent in playing challenging compositions and demanding jazz standards. With our phones and cameras, we captured them in action. We then shared these clips with our family, especially their near-age cousins. Moreover, we voiced our astonishment with the bands' performances and their role in each group. We are confident they both finished the evening feeling good about their musical skills and budding competence as teenagers and musicians.

They Want Feedback about
Their Emerging Talents, Skills, and Dispositions

Grandchildren benefit significantly from positive feedback provided by grandparents. As we affirm their developing talents, skills, and dispositions, they come to understand who they are and what they might become. Our feedback helps them want to succeed. It helps them persist in practicing and improving their knowledge and skillsets. Moreover, our affirmations support the emergence of valuable dispositions such as fairness, persistence, teamwork, kindness, inclusion, and a host of other valuable character traits.

💡 Recently, we attended a fundraiser for a children's hospital. Together with other musicians, one of our granddaughters performed at this fundraising event as a part of the entertainment. She sang three songs while playing her guitar. We videotaped her and then promptly sent the video clips to other family members for their enjoyment. It was evident that our attendance and attention meant a great deal to her. Several hours later, we sent her a text conveying our delight, praising her increased skill as a musician and her willingness to contribute to this fundraising event.

Even if you live great distances from your grandchildren, you can be exceptionally interested in their emerging talents. You do this by establishing regular times for communicating and finding out what they are doing. Your sources of information are your grandchildren and their parents. When you Skype, talk on the phone, text, or receive photos or videos of your grandchildren performing, use these sources of information to express your awe, respect, praise, or excitement for how they are growing, improving, and maturing. Send them texts, write them letters, talk with them directly—anything that allows you to deliver personal, positive feedback. In the absence of your feedback, grandchildren must rely exclusively on their appraisals, which may be inaccurate and less motivational. Just think of your own experiences receiving positive feedback from a peer, coworker, or boss. Small amounts of authentic praise and affirmation are immensely satisfying and motivational to grandchildren.

They Want to Feel Confident and Have a Sense of Control

One of the greatest gifts you can give your grandchildren is a sense of confidence, a feeling that they can make good choices and have the power to put them into action. Few things are worse than feeling insecure, powerless, or out of control.

You show your trust by encouraging them to act for themselves. You say things like this: "This is your decision. This is your choice. You have what it takes to come up with excellent solutions to this problem. I am happy to be a consultant, but the choice is yours. You can do this!

They Want to Feel Significant

When we say grandkids want to feel significant, we mean this: They want to feel loved. When you feel loved, you experience powerful feelings of acceptance and support. You feel wanted, needed, and connected. To state the obvious, feeling loved, really loved, is the sublime source of everything beautiful in everyone's life. As you insightfully and wisely respond to your grandchildren's needs, they will feel significant, they will feel loved!

They Want Advice and Counsel, But Only When They Request It

As grandchildren mature and move into their late teens and young-adult years, you will be sought out occasionally for advice and counsel if you have established excellent relationships of trust. The help they seek may be related to schooling, emerging relationships, challenges in a work environment, or significant decisions.

In giving advice and counsel, you must first come to understand the nature of the issues with which they are dealing. Again, unhurried listening, accompanied with real intent, is vital. Take the appropriate time to ensure that you understand what they are seeking in the way of advice. You will know you are on the right track if you employ these kinds of questions: "Let me see if I have this right—are you concerned about _____?" "Am I correct in assuming that this is the challenge you are facing?" "Would it be safe to say that you are primarily concerned with this issue?" Using questions like these will position you to give useful advice.

💡 Several weeks ago, a grandson gave me a call. I could tell he was anxious and eager to get some ideas and advice dealing with the doldrums of selling, door-to-door, pest control. From our conversation, I could tell that he was looking for ideas that would help him approach his selling activities with more confidence and creativity. We spoke for almost an hour. He asked me what I did when my motivation for engaging in a vital activity flat-lined or was about to evaporate. I did my best to share practices I used to improve my mood and behavior, including listing to music, using more accurate self-talk, choosing to be more creative, stepping out of the usual sales pitch routines, regularly exercising, and giving myself appropriate diversions to recharge. I think I was helpful to him. We ended our phone conversation with the customary, "I love you." He finished his summer sales work and learned a lot about himself, his work, and the value of persistence.

They Want High-Quality Relationships

As we have stated many times, positive relationships are at the heart of grandparenting on purpose. They contribute mightily to the influence we can have on our grandchildren and their parents. The impact we wish to exert is not meant to be manipulative. It is intended to be genuinely helpful, supportive, therapeutic, and useful to our grandchildren and their parents.

Our relationships allow us to contribute to the development of our grandchildren—who they become, what they might value, and what contributions they might wish to make during their lifetimes. These connections also put us in a position to be truly helpful and to be sought out when our grandchildren and their parents encounter challenges and problems. The benefits of these connections are many, so do everything you can to establish them.

🔆 Some years ago, one of our daughters and her husband experienced significant stress with a daughter who had substantial anxiety issues. As she began her first week of junior high, she was overwhelmed with considerable fears and anxiety. School for her was synonymous with potential injury, harm, and extreme emotional stress. No amount of encouragement, praise, or promised rewards on the part of her parents or others motivated her to go to school and attend classes.

Early one morning during this first week of school, I remember receiving a call from her mother, asking me to come to their home. It was a call for help. She was desperate. Her daughter was again resisting her mother's attempts to get her to go to school. She refused to leave her bedroom.

This granddaughter had never struggled with anything during her elementary-school years. She enjoyed going to school. She excelled academically. She never missed school-related activities in any form. However, her behaviors in response to beginning her junior-high years were perplexing and emotionally draining for all.

Fortunately, I had established a great relationship with this granddaughter. She trusted me. She never refused to do anything I had asked her to do if the request seemed reasonable and right. When I arrived at their home, apprehension and worry permeated the whole house. I thought if our granddaughter is refusing to comply with her mother's requests, how will she respond to me?

With some mild encouragement, I was able to take her to school. During the subsequent weeks and months of this first year of junior high, her parents, a talented school counselor, and a caring special educator were able to address the challenges of her extreme anxiety. All of us worked collaboratively in nurturing this talented, bright, and capable girl. She eventually went to school willingly and energetically.

For the remainder of her seventh-grade year, I picked her up every Thursday at the end of the school day. We traveled to our nearby home to work on various projects—cleaning our refrigerator, weeding, dusting, etc. These projects spawned a lot of informal conversations and sharing. She was able to talk about her anxiety and a host of other things. Our working together cemented my relationship with her.

She still has anxiety issues, but she is learning how to deal with them. She is now confident in doing many things that earlier she completely and resolutely would have avoided.

> My visits with grandpa were just what I needed in junior high. It gave me a safe space to share my thoughts and fears with someone I trusted. Grandpa's love and encouragement to go to school were monumental in getting over my anxieties and fears. He was there to celebrate every success, no matter how small or silly. I definitely would not be where I am today without the wisdom and guidance I received from my grandpa in junior high.
>
> *Abby, Granddaughter, 20*

They Want Boundaries
(Sometimes They Want Them, and Other Times They Don't)

Boundaries are rules or standards of conduct that have consequences, both positive and negative. These rules/boundaries focus on helping grandchildren know what to expect in various settings—your home, car, etc. Children and youth generally feel safer and more confident when they know what the rules and boundaries are.

We begin special events, long-term stays at our home, or other related activities with clear expectations and rules. They may be as straightforward as these:

- We solve issues by talking, not fighting.
- We honor agreed-upon rules.
- We are responsible—we clean up the messes we make.

- We help with the preparation, serving, and cleanup of meals.
- We let others know where we are going.
- When issues surface, we solve problems—we find win-win solutions.
- We respect others' items, toys, and other belongings.
- We listen.
- We learn from our experiences and mistakes.

These are boundaries we have used to help our grandchildren grow and develop into caring and responsible individuals.

One of our best creations for family retreats and cabin stays is our "Cleanup Teams." We spoke of these teams earlier. Rather than have the adults do all of the cleanup, garbage removal, and other duties, we have groups of grandchildren/cousins who work together to clean up after meals. They wash dishes, scour pans, clean grills, dry and put away dishes, remove the garbage, and sweep floors. We specify what needs to be done following each meal. These teams have been remarkably helpful in fostering responsibility and teaching valuable skills to our grandchildren. They learn how to work in teams and how to share workloads. This process has become something that they look forward to and accomplish with a lot of laughter, joking, and enthusiasm.

They Want Informal and Meaningful Experiences

Our grandchildren love intimate experiences that naturally give rise to conversations, discussions, and friendship development. Most often, these experiences involve food preparation or cookie making. When grandchildren gather around a table for something to eat, they effortlessly begin to talk and share what is going on in their lives. The same is true of events that include board or yard games. Notably, younger grandchildren derive significant benefits from these gatherings or events. They see and learn first-hand what it means to talk with others, share experiences, and express opinions.

💡 We regularly host what we refer to as College Kids' Night. Our grandchildren and their friends gather for an evening of food and fun. They invite their friends. It begins with an easy-to-prepare meal followed by a brief, stimulating media piece. Sometimes, we watch a Technology, Entertainment, and Design (TED) talk or presentation. Sometimes we watch an engaging, vintage movie. Other times, they just hang out and play various games. We end the evening with a dessert. These gatherings are particularly popular during the summer.

One of the most entertaining of these evenings was one that was held just before Valentine's Day. We watched a TED Talk focused on the topic of rejection.*

The assembled grandkids and their friends loved the talk. The resultant group discussion was not only fun but also instructive. Each participant left the evening, having enjoyed a great meal. Moreover, each left with a better understanding of how to interpret and respond to rejection. Also, many left feeling more connected with cousins and associated friends.

---

*Jia Jiang: *What I Learned from 100 Days of Rejection,* https://www .youtube.com/watch?v=ZFWyseydTkQ.

One thing special about my relationship with my grandpa is that he knows and is interested in everything going on in my life, but my friends' lives as well. Grandpa Winn makes an effort to get to know all the people in my life and make them feel loved and important. They love being invited to dinner or given cookies.

Eliza, Granddaughter, 21

They Want to Know Who They Are

Grandchildren derive a lot of satisfaction knowing their roots and learning about their grandparents, great-grandparents, and others who preceded them. Most are very curious about their origins. From what lands and regions of the world did their ancestors come? What stories are available about the lives and experiences of their forebears?

We come from Irish, English, Scandinavian, and African roots. Several of our siblings have returned to their homelands to the very cities from which our ancestors came. We also have access to several first-person journals that recount the history of our progenitors. These journals and other family-history records help grandchildren have a context for their lives and help them discover what courage and grit were needed to make their present lives possible and full of opportunities.

Our grandchildren and our children have been especially touched by one journal, particular*ly Pioneering the West.*** This published journal reveals much about early life in the western United States. Its stories uncover a great deal about the early pioneers, the Pony Express, Native Americans,

---

**His Thrilling Experiences among the Indians* by Howard Egan (Springville, UT: Cedar Fort, Inc., 2008).

and exciting historical events on the edges of the emerging United States. Our children and their children love this book and others written by their ancestors. These journals and related stories give them a sense of who they are. They help them discover why they do certain things well and how they might mirror some of the resilience of their forbearers. Current, easy-to-use, online resources make exploring your family history possible and thoroughly enjoyable.*

Now that you have had time to explore our beliefs about what grandchildren want. Let's talk about what they overwhelmingly need. Intriguingly, we believe their wants and needs are the same. Grandchildren need quality connections. They need to be heard and understood. They need authenticity—to mention only a few. The exceedingly good news is this: when we consistently meet the wants and needs of grandchildren illuminated in this chapter, grandchildren thrive and eventually become the adults, parents, neighbors, associates, and citizens our communities and country so desperately need.

---

*See www.ancestry.com, www.myheritage.com, and www.findmy past.com.

How could you improve your connections with each grandchild or just one of your grandchildren?

_____

_____

_____

_____

_____

_____

_____

_____

_____

Some of topics explored in this chapter are listening, being authentic, being engaged and involved, giving advice, establishing boundaries, providing structured experiences, and coming to know your heritage—what steps seem to make sense on any of these fronts?

_____

_____

_____

_____

_____

_____

_____

_____

_____

What will be your next step or initiative with your grandchildren or with one grandchild?

_____

_____

_____

_____

_____

_____

_____

_____

_____

_____

_____

Chapter 10

Wrap Up

Significant Ideas and Practices: A Summary

Thank you for your persistence! And kudos to you for wanting to become a purposeful grandparent! This chapter provides a brief summary of many of the significant ideas and practices presented in the book. It is also a booster shot of sorts—a means for quickly reviewing some of the essential concepts you have learned and considered.

We genuinely hope the stories we have shared with you have been useful and even a little inspirational. Our stories were primarily designed to get you thinking about what would work in your own family. We hope they will serve as springboards for actions tailored to your family.

As you moved through the book, we hope you consistently avoided the comparison trap. Always remember no contrasts! No two families are identical. Each family has its own needs and distinctive characteristics. Your grandparenting on purpose needs to be tailored to your family. We are counting on you to be inventive in designing your practices, traditions, and routines, and modifying them as your family needs change.

Responsible and Caring Grandchildren

Few things in life exceed the splendor of having grand-children who have chosen to become reliable and caring human beings. When grandchildren have a keen sense of who they are, when they know how to work hard, when they have developed courage, when they know how to nurture others, when they have become inclusive, and when they have developed resilience, we know they will contribute much to their own eventual families, neighborhoods, and communities. Ultimately, they will become the kind of parents and grandparents their children and grandchildren want and need.

> I want to be a loving grandparent. Because this is what I have grown up with, and I really appreciate the love and support my grandparents have shown me.
>
> *Dane, 15*

> I want to be just like g-ma. She would interact with us as much she could and never missed out on things she knew she could attend. I also want to be like my grandpa by being optimistic. He is good at uplifting others and taking pictures of my teammates and me. He then shares the images with them and me. His puns make everyone giggle. I want to be like them because they make my cousins and me better people, and I want to do that for my grandchildren.
>
> *Livie, 14*

> I want to be just like my sweet grandparents. I want to be loving, fun, informative, happy, and supportive.

I also want to be involved in each of my grandchildren's lives—no matter what the circumstances.

Maggie, Granddaughter, 20

We love our grandchildren and their parents. Hopefully, you have sensed our concern and our desire to be genuinely helpful to you. We want you to be successful as you create and sustain positive relationships with your grandchildren and their parents. Likewise, we want you to enjoy your sacred calling and work as a grandparent.

Making a Difference

We know grandparents can make enormous and positive differences in the lives of their grandchildren. Such was the case for our children. During their formative years, they lived next door to their Egan grandparents, who engaged them in all kinds of meaningful activities and conversations. We will always be grateful for their influence in nurturing our children. We hope you remember with clarity the influential role Linda's grandmother played in supporting her as a teenager and young adult. Grandma Rhoda made a significant difference in the quality and trajectory of her life.

Let's take some time to review where we have been together. Let's consider some of the core principles that support and serve as the foundation for our work as purposeful grandparents.

Being Purposeful and Deliberate

Purposeful and deliberate grandparents focus on contributing positively to their grandchildren and their parents. They have definite ideas of what they wish to achieve and develop in their grandchildren. Fundamentally, they are committed to the happiness of their grandchildren and their parents. They know that making a difference in the lives of those they love the most depends primarily on the positive relationships they have established and sustained with each family member.

> My grandparents are my closest and dearest friends. I think this is rare. This is the result of the purposeful, thoughtful effort my grandparents have injected into our relationship. My grandparents have made themselves available to me in almost every way. I remember them supporting me at all my special moments growing up. I have many memories of quick texts professing their love and encouragement. We've played music, football, and braved mountains together. Even when I've made mistakes, I've felt comfortable to discuss every detail with them, holding nothing back. I think that's the magic of my grandparents. My grandparents make me feel so comfortable, so at peace, so undeniably free to be myself with no judgment. They accept me for who I am and love me unconditionally. It's something special, and I feel lucky to be the receiver of that kind of love.
>
> *Emma, Granddaughter, 22*

What is the takeaway from this section! Make your relationships count! If your ties are weak or altogether lacking, take the recommended steps to repair and rebuild them. Get reconnected!

No Comparisons, Just Springboards

We expressed some strong recommendations at the beginning of the book. We restate them again, believing that following them is central to your continuing success and growth as a grandparent. Just remember, *no comparisons!* Each of us is different. Each of us has diverse talents and dispositions. We all come with baggage, our own unique experiences, and our distinctive motivations and knowledge about grandparenting. Given these differences, stay away from any comparisons with us or anyone else in your friendship circle. As you reflect on your successes (and perhaps a few failures or missteps), be kind to yourself. Be reasonable. Be realistic. Simply have a growth perspective. If you are growing, make that the basis for determining and measuring your success.

Creating Positive Relationships

Building and sustaining positive relationships is a function of consistently knowing and responding in helpful and responsible ways to your grandchildren and their parents' needs. Purposeful grandparents are skilled in discovering and meeting some, but not all, the needs of their grandchildren. Some of you serve as backup or substitute parents for your children, assisting and contributing as you are inspired and directed. For some grandchildren, you are their parents. In all that you do, focus most of your efforts on creating positive relationships with your grandchildren and their parents.

Accessing Inspiration

We cannot overstate the importance of inspiration in our sacred work and calling as grandparents. As we indicated, you are entitled to light and guidance—lots of it. Light and guidance present themselves in many ways and come in many forms. Fundamentally, they provide direction, help, and ideas so you can be confident in your attempts to be responsive to the needs of your grandchildren and their parents. Often this light comes from meditating, pondering, or prayer. It also comes from caring friends, professionals, and colleagues. Our only obligation is to seek it, be responsive to its impressions, and be grateful for its presence and mighty power to enable good things.

We Shared Our Best Practices

We know that not everything we shared with you was helpful with your unique circumstances. We also know that we are atypical—over the top—when it comes to being grandparents. Thank you for your patience and understanding.

Because we all come to grandparenting with widely diverse backgrounds, experiences, and preparation, it's impossible to prepare a book that speaks entirely and individually to each grandparent's needs. This said, we hope the ideas, routines, traditions, and other things we shared with you were sufficient to get you started and motivated. We hope they serve as springboards for your family activities and practices.

We are committed to a long-term relationship with you. We have created a website, **grandparentingonpurpose.com**, where we will continue to share helpful ideas and practices that emanate from you and other grandparents. We want to know about your triumphs and your challenges. Please let us hear from you. This website will be a place where you can pose questions, share your experiences, and look for new ideas, routines, and traditions.

Vitally Important Roles of Grandparents

As you will recall from chapter 1, the roles and functions of grandparents are many and varied. We suggested that highly effective grandparents are great listeners, committed relationship specialists, problem solvers, talent developers, long-term investors, and savvy event planners, among other things.

> I love how my grandparents teach us to love each other and to appreciate the time we get to spend together. They always are planning family events, activities, and dinners and encouraging us to connect with each other. As I've grown older, I've learned to value these events and look forward to the conversations and experiences I get to have with my grandparents and cousins.
>
> *Eliza, Granddaughter, 21*

In the months to come, you may want to revisit some of the chapters to see how you have grown as a grandparent.

Coming to Know Your Grandchildren's Needs

In chapter 2, we suggested actions grandparents might take to identify and remain sensitive to their grandchildren and their parents' needs. If you are a careful observer, if you listen carefully and look for what your grandchildren are feeling, you will know their needs. To refresh your memory, let's revisit some questions that you should be able to answer:

- What do you know individually about your grandchildren?
- What are their capacities?
- What are their strengths?
- What are their passions?
- What are their challenges?
- What are their aspirations?

- What do they thoroughly enjoy doing with you?
- Who are their closest friends?
- Who are the other vital adults in their lives?
- What foods do they love?
- What music do they like?
- How do they like school?
- What is just one thing you could do to bring some joy into each of their lives?

If you know the answers to many of these questions, you are well on your way to addressing your grandchildren's needs.

Connecting with Grandchildren

In chapter 3 and elsewhere, we highlighted activities for connecting with grandchildren both near and far. We began with the Jacob Books, interactive books that were sent between families detailing the experiences of a very young grandson and the activities of each set of his grandparents. Of course, the Jacob Books predated the development of social media, which are now so easy to use. Still, there is something special about having a real book in your hands. Even now, we love thumbing through the Jacob Book pages, seeing what we were doing during his early years. We also identified other means for linking with grandchildren in this chapter, including two of our favorites: postcards and birthday letters.

The postcards are and have been one of our greatest successes in involving our grandchildren. They loved receiving something addressed to them from a city or country far from their home.

Birthday letters, by their very nature, have significant bonding powers. These letters are immediately opened and read. These letters don't need to qualify as "literature." Just write as you would talk to your grandchildren. Their content is such that they appeal to each grandchild. In these letters, we find ways to deliver positive feedback about who they are becoming. We share with them what we like about their actions and achievements of the past year. We identify the funny things we have observed about them. We affirm emerging talents and positive dispositions. Moreover, we suggest ideas that they may want to give attention to as they move through the upcoming year. We provide small bits of counsel and advice—not too much and not too little.

Mary Jane, one of our granddaughters, recently suggested that we bind each grandchild's birthday letters, making them into small books that would be given to grandchildren as wedding gifts. What a terrific idea! We have all or most of their letters from the time they could barely read to the present. We agree they would be cherished gifts.

Facing Real Challenges

In chapter 4, we spoke to the challenges, realities, and serious problems that some grandparents face attempting to initiate and sustain positive relationships with their children and their spouses. Given our conversations with dear friends and associates, we know that some children and their spouses pose significant barriers to establishing connections with them or their children. We hope we were modestly successful in helping you determine whether any actions or attempts might produce favorable results to connect with your children and their companions. We welcome your input on this and other topics of concern on our website, grandparentingonpursose.com.

Traditions and Routines

Chapter 5 was remarkably easy for us to write. We presented several ongoing traditions that our grandchildren and their parents genuinely like.

We hope the sharing of our family traditions (Christmas Car Races, "Chicken-Fish" Sandwiches, and Cheap, But Really Good Dinners) was helpful to you and gave you some ideas about what would work in your family.

Chapter 6, Family Routines, inspired many positive memories for us. As you recall, family routines are miniature versions of family traditions. They are the little, repetitive practices we do in our family. They give structure and meaning to family life. If we had to focus on one, it would be regular, family meals accompanied by natural and meaningful conversations about what is happening in your grandchildren's and their parents' lives.

Yearly Themes

Chapter 7 described our attempts to help our grandchildren and their parents focus on highly valuable dispositions and associated behaviors. These themes centered on manners, learning to be courageous, learning to do hard things, reaching out to others, and being generous—to mention just a few. Through these themes, we have endeavored to make it clear to our grandchildren what behaviors and dispositions we value as grandparents.

Building Spirituality

Chapter 8 was our attempt to speak about nurturing spirituality in our grandchildren. We stressed the importance of reflecting spirituality in our lives, since nothing trumps the power and profound influence of example. We attempted to define what spirituality is and how central it is to experiencing and enjoying a purposeful life. We then proceeded to talk about what we have done to build and nurture it in our grandchildren.

We believe spirituality is at the heart of helping our grandchildren experience meaningful and fulfilling lives. It presents itself in many ways, including service to others, guidance in making important decisions, and sharing light and generosity with family members, neighbors, and other sojourners on earth. Lastly, it is a divine source of inspiration, influence, guidance, and healing.

What Do Grandchildren Want and Need?

In writing chapter 9, we wanted to create a capstone for the book. This chapter spoke directly about our thoughts regarding the wants and needs of grandchildren. We know that connecting with grandchildren and their parents is an intensively personal and rewarding process. Positive and enduring relationships come from purposeful, intentional, and deliberate actions centered on meeting the wholesome wants and needs of your grandchildren and their parents. You do this by laying down "connective tissues" that bind you together as individuals and families. As you consistently embrace the principles and recommended practices in *Grandparenting on Purpose,* you will experience greater happiness and fulfillment in your sacred role as a grandparent. Also, your grandkids and their parents will be happier too.

Cautions and Advice

Be patient with your attempts to become a more purposeful grandparent. Remember, grandchildren and their parents are very skilled authenticity detectors. Whatever you do, make sure your grandparenting is done with sincerity and integrity. If grandchildren know your intentions are authentic, they will be more likely to go along with you and support your efforts to motivate their growth and success.

Have a growth mentality. Enjoy becoming the kind of grandparent your grandchildren want and need. And please stay in touch at grandparentingonpurpose.com! We want to hear from you!

 **Recipes**

Egan Clam Dip

Preparation time: 15 minutes
Servings: 4–8 depending on the ages and appetites of the dippers

Ingredients List

Cream cheese (16 ounces)
Juice of 1 lemon or to taste
1 can minced clams (6.5 ounces) with clam juice
Pepper
Corn Chips 15½ ounces

Preparation

1. Let the cream cheese soften to room temperature.
2. Add the softened cream cheese to bowl that will accommodate an eggbeater and protect you from flying food debris.
3. Drain the clams, save the juice.
4. Combine the clams and softened cream cheese.
5. Add clam juice incrementally until you have the consistency you like.
6. Add lemon juice and pepper to taste.
7. Place close to a bowl of corn chips and let the conversations and dipping begin.

Egan Punch

Preparation time: 5–10 minutes
Servings: 8–12 depending on the ages and appetites of your grandchildren

Ingredients List
2-liter bottle of lemon-lime soda
2 liters orange juice
2 tablespoons grenadine syrup
Ice

Preparation
1. Combine equal amounts of soda and orange juice
2. Add the grenadine syrup to achieve the color you prefer. We prefer a drink that is neither bright orange nor deep red—something in between.
3. Add ice to the serving pitcher or cups.
4. Then enjoy this unusual tasting combination that may become your own family punch.
5. Also, enjoy lots of high-quality conversations between sips of punch.
6. Best enjoyed with rooms without white carpet.

Lake-Powell Hash

Preparation time: 20–30 minutes
Servings: 10–12 servings

Ingredients List

1 (32 ounce) package of frozen, hash brown potatoes.
1 (12 ounce) can of Spam
6–8 eggs
Butter or oil
Favorite salsa or ketchup
Salt and pepper

Preparation

1. Prepare potatoes as directed on the packaging with a large skillet.

2. While the potatoes are cooking, cut the Spam into ¼ inch cubes.

3. Brown the cubes of Spam in a separate pan.

4. Wisk the eggs in a small bowl and then add them to the hash brown/Spam mixture.

5. Scramble the eggs until they are cooked to the desired doneness.

6. Salt and pepper to taste.

7. Serve with salsa or ketchup.

Grandpa Winn's Oatmeal Chocolate Chip Cookies

Preparation time: 15-20 minutes
Servings: 48 using a small 1¾ inch ice-cream scoop.

Ingredients List

8 ounces softened butter

3 large eggs

1 cup brown sugar

1 cup granulated sugar

2 teaspoons baking soda

½ teaspoon baking powder

¼ teaspoon salt

2 tablespoons vanilla

Flour or flour substitute, 2 cups [gluten free: 4–5 cups of almond flour)

4 cups regular oats

½ cup steel-cut oats (they make the cookies crunchier)

36-ounce package milk chocolate chips

Preparation

1. Preheat oven to 375 degrees.

2. Make room in your oven for two trays or racks of cookies.

3. 18 x 13-inch cookie sheets with parchment paper

4. Combine the softened butter, eggs, brown and granulated sugar, baking soda, baking powder, salt, and vanilla until smooth.

5. Add the flour, followed by the oats and steel-cut oats.

6. Add the milk chocolate chips.

7. Thoroughly stir all the ingredients together.

8. Using a 1¾ inch cookie or ice cream scoop, drop cookie dough on parchment-lined cookie sheets.

9. Bake for 13–15 minutes, depending on your oven. The second rack of cookies may need to cook a little longer.

10. Remove cookies to a cooling rack or countertop.

11. Get out some cold milk, and enjoy yourself!

"Chicken-Fish" Sandwiches

Preparation time: 10 minutes
Servings: 5–7 depending on the bun or bread size

Ingredients List
    1 (12.5) ounce can white chicken
    Mayonnaise to taste
    Dill pickles or whatever your preference is
    Lettuce
    Bread or buns
    Potato chips or corn chips

Preparation
    1. Mix the chicken with the mayonnaise.
    2. Add small chunks of pickles.
    3. Prepare sandwiches with lettuce.
    4. Serve with your favorite potato or corn chips.
    5. Have some great conversations!

 # Note to the Reader

Don't miss out! Here is our invitation to grow with us. Join our community of curious and caring grandparents. Link and learn with us in discovering powerful practices and ideas for connecting with your grandchildren. Our promise is simply this: You will improve your relationships with your children and their spouses. You will have more fun as a grandparent and so will your grandchildren. Go to our website: grandparentingonpurpose.com. Visit our blog to find some of the best things you can do with your grandchildren right now. You will not be disappointed.

 **About the Authors**

Linda and I grew up within blocks of each other. It was not until we entered high school that we became friends. I dated her a few times during my senior year. Following 30 months of church-centered service; I returned home and began to actively date Linda again. A little more than a year later, we were married. Now 50-plus years later, we have four married children, one son and three daughters (Daniel and Kristin, Amy Dott and Scott, Mary Ann and Ryan, as well as Marcia and David). They have given us 22 fun-loving and caring grandchildren. Early in 2019, Linda, my loving companion, passed away from complications of several chronic conditions. We sorely miss her matchless light and love. From the very outset of our grandparenting, Linda and I focused our best efforts on building and sustaining loving relationships with each grandchild and their parents. Thereafter, we directed our efforts at contributing to their happiness and success. This book chronicles our best efforts to be purposeful and caring grandparents.

Printed in Great Britain
by Amazon